Issues in
ACADEMIC
FREEDOM

edited by George S. Worgul, Jr.

Duquesne University Press
Pittsburgh, Pennsylvania

Published in the United States of America

by Duquesne University Press
600 Forbes Avenue
Pittsburgh, Pennsylvania 15282–0101

Library of Congress Cataloging-in-Publication Data
Issues in academic freedom/edited by George S. Worgul, Jr.
    p. cm.
    Includes bibliographical references (p.).
    ISBN 0-8207-0237-4:
    1. Academic freedom. 2. Academic freedom—United States.
3. Catholic universities and colleges. 4. Catholic universities
and colleges—United States.   I. Worgul, George S.
LC72.I85   1992
378.1'21—dc20   92–1039
                                                       CIP

Contents

Editor's Preface

The dawning of Christianity's second millennium finds Catholicism engaged in a search for identity. Once again the church faces the challenge of new people, new contexts and new issues. History's forward march will not permit ecclesial immobility. The church must take up the perennial task of examining who it is and how it is to accomplish its mission or run the risk of being judged irrelevant.

While each new age presents its own questions and crises, there are periods where the challenge issued is more substantive, intensive and pervasive. These are the eras when the church is confronted with the dramatic shift of cultural worldviews. The change from the god-centered classic/medieval culture to the human-centered enlightenment culture was such a time. Almost every indicator available suggests that the current era is a similar epoch of intense transformation and the gradual emergence of a new worldview. The enlightenment's unconscious presupposition of autonomous reason's self-sufficiency and self-finality has proved to be wanting. Social patterns of behavior and institutions built on this presupposition are crumbling. A worldview is being constructed that relocates reason within the expansive range of human gifts, talents and faculties. The rediscovery of values, spirituality, ethics, emotions, intuition, imagination, and human community are all shaping the global vision that is being born.

If the church is to discover its identity in a climate of cultural transformation, it must be keenly sensitive to life as experienced both within and without its community. The exact shape and form of the emerging culture remains hidden. At present we can only detect tendencies and trajectories. Surely, it will be a worldview that embraces pluralism, that is concerned for the cosmos and ecological systems, that strives to order a social life with respect for human rights and dignity. It will be truly *global* worldview that recognizes that commerce, politics, education, health systems, etc., are interwoven both within a nation and across the nations of the world.

Where might the church turn in its effort to understand this "world in the making" and explore its identity and mission in this world? The university, in particular the Catholic university, may well be the resource most adequately equipped for this project. Catholic universities exist to foster and enrich the interchange and dialogue between faith and all of human knowing. In this context, the church can more deeply understand how truth, value and meaning, mediated by every human inquiry, can deepen the understanding of Christian faith and how Christians might best live this faith in the myriad choices that must be made in life's ever increasing complexity. Simultaneously, the different fields and disciplines of human inquiry can be challenged by Christian claims about God, people and the meaning of life.

The identification of Catholic Universities as critical resources in an age of deep cultural transformation should not be interpreted as a simple elixir to a serious challenge. Some have suggested that the title *Catholic university* is an oxymoron. They argue that a true university must be "free" and that Catholic universities are too limited by their ecclesial relationships to enjoy the necessary "academic freedom" that constitutes true university enterprise. This criticism might be answered by demonstrating that "academic freedom" at any university—whether public, private, church-related or church-sponsored—is never unlimited or absolute. Every university has an identity and mission to which it must adhere. Every faculty member has a responsibility to the methods of their discipline and the warrants the discipline establishes as required as relatively adequate for "truth claims." Freedom is always a situated freedom and a responsible freedom.

While a prima facie rejection of the very possibility of Catholic universities on the basis of "academic freedom" might be critiqued as myopic, nonetheless it does identify issues and questions about the nature of Catholic universities that must be explored and answered. The present volume addresses the central issue: academic freedom at a Catholic university. The texts offer insight and analysis of various dimensions of the issue from different positions of responsibility, e.g., university president, faculty member or Catholic bishop. The essays approach the issue from both theory and personal experience, from a North American and a European context, and from the concerns of systematic theology and the interest of ethics. Three of the essays (Murray, Byron, Dulles) were originally drafted as papers for the symposium, "Academic Freedom in a Pluralistic Society," at Duquesne University, Pittsburgh. The other essays were specifically commissioned for this volume.

1 • A Right to Dissent: American or Catholic?
Ethical Reflections on Academic Freedom

James P. Hanigan

The heated discussion and often painful dissension in the American Catholic community, provoked by what the Jesuit publication *America* called *L'Affaire Curran*,[1] may well be somewhat clouded for many American Catholics, and simply incomprehensible to non-Catholics, due to the fact that it is taking place in a context of U.S. political and civic values. The Vatican's expulsion of a highly esteemed theological scholar from his tenured position at the Catholic University of America was certainly awkward, and even embarrassing, for many American Catholics who regarded it as a flagrant transgression of personal rights as well as an obvious violation of academic freedom.[2]

The dismissal of Father Charles E. Curran was linked

1

in the minds of Catholic critics to the prior insistence in the new Code of Canon Law that all teachers of theological disciplines in Catholic colleges and universities be required to have a canonical mandate,[3] as well as to the norms for governing Catholic institutions of higher learning suggested in the "Proposed Schema for a Pontifical Document on Catholic Universities" from the Vatican Congregation for Catholic Education.[4] Subsequent Vatican documents from the Congregation for the Doctrine of the Faith, most notably the "Profession of Faith and Oath of Fidelity"[5] and the "Instruction on the Ecclesial Vocation of the Theologian"[6] further troubled those American Catholics who had thought the days of Roman authoritarianism and censorship, manifested clearly in its seeming disregard for traditional liberal freedoms and due process, were behind them.

The rights of every individual person to freedom of opinion, speech, press and association, all intimately linked to the more basic rights of freedom of conscience and of religious liberty,[7] are so much taken for granted in the American social context that any apparent challenge to them is met with an almost instinctive hostility by those sensitive to the challenge. Such challenges are instantly rejected as unfair infringements on individual human rights. Consequently, they are often interpreted as nothing more than self-serving power plays by a threatened authoritarian bureaucracy. To interpret the present struggle over personal rights and especially over academic freedom in Catholic colleges and universities in this way, however, seems to me both confusing and false.[8]

Not all American Catholics, of course, were of the above opinion. A considerable number of Catholics felt that Rome's statements and actions in regard to Catholic colleges and universities and their faculties were long overdue and necessary to correct an unhealthy and divisive pluralism in the Catholic Church. Many who held this view saw the illness[9] to be most manifest in an Americanization of the church that smacked more of

Protestantism than Catholicism. On this accounting, theologians were setting themselves up as an alternate, independent magisterium or teaching office, and introducing an incoherent pluralism into Catholic doctrine and life, thereby confusing the faithful, harming the unity of the church and striking at its hierarchical constitution.[10] Liberal rights and democratic processes were all very well and good in the political order but had at best an auxiliary place in the life of the church and its various institutional activities.

There is most certainly a doctrine and an appreciation of human rights in the Roman Catholic theological tradition that has been renewed rather vigorously in the writings of the popes since John XXIII, in the documents of the Second Vatican Council, as well as in the work of theologians.[11] This tradition of thought prizes rights as fundamental and essential safeguards of human dignity and insists upon their social institutionalization and protection.[12] But this tradition does not understand rights in quite the same way as the American political tradition does, nor does it value them for quite the same reasons. Most importantly, the Catholic tradition does not always recognize what is required for their institutional embodiment and protection.[13] A clarification of these differences in understanding and evaluation should not only shed some light on what is going on in the present situation of conflict between the hierarchy and theologians, but should also help us arrive at a properly ethical understanding of academic freedom.

ACADEMIC FREEDOM AND DISSENT: A SECULAR VIEW

Philosophically and constitutionally, as well as in actual practice, academic freedom is neither a simple reality nor a clearly agreed upon concept.[14] The same can be said for the concepts of ethics and rights.[15] Despite this conceptual and practical confusion, however, academic freedom in the American context is widely construed as an individual right, as an extension and application of the rights to freedom of opinion, speech and press appropriate to professors in colleges and universities.[16] The subject or claimant of the freedom called academic is said to be the individual faculty member, the person who is employed by the institution to carry out the tasks of teaching and research. It has been the faculty member, as the subject of academic freedom, who has been the exclusive focus of attention in most theoretical and practical discussions of academic freedom by academic professionals, as can be seen in the now classic definition of academic freedom by Arthur Lovejoy.

> Academic freedom is the freedom of the teacher or research worker in higher institutions of learning to investigate and discuss the problems of his science and to express his conclusions, whether through publications or in the instruction of students without interference from political or ecclesiastical authority, or from the administrative officials of the institution in which he is employed, unless his methods are found by qualified bodies of his own profession to be clearly incompetent or contrary to professional ethics.[17]

The same focus has been continued in the widely accepted "Statement of Principles on Academic Freedom and Tenure" of the American Association of University Professors (AAUP).[18]

There are good reasons for this primary focus on the individual faculty member as the bearer of the right of academic freedom, since it is the faculty that carries out most immediately and directly the specific tasks for which colleges and universities exist. It is the faculty, individually and collectively, that most clearly embodies what the academic institution is about, whose professional specializations give it its distinctive character and whose competence and professional achievements are a major measure of its level of excellence.

Understood as Lovejoy has defined it in individual and

somewhat formal terms, the freedom that is called academic is a *negative right*,[19] an immunity claim to noninterference in the practice of one's social role and so in the pursuit and realization of the goods intrinsic to that practice.[20] The claim to immunity from interference is directed against social authorities both external and internal to the academic institution. This conveys the impression, at least, that it is social authority, and perhaps even society itself,[21] which is the major enemy of academic freedom, and that academic freedom has its clearest test and guarantee when a faculty member is free to dissent from the established wisdom and policies of state, church or the academic administration without fear of reprisal. Interestingly enough, the claim to noninterference is not made against one's professional peers and colleagues, nor is it leveled against the economic benefactors of the institution. The scholar's academic freedom has two accepted limits: methods of teaching and inquiry can be judged to be clearly incompetent by one's professional colleagues, or professional ethics can be violated.

A number of observations about this understanding of academic freedom are germane. First, it is clearly an individualistic conception of freedom, an attempt to carve out a private space for the scholar against the all-too-likely incursions of political, ecclesiastical or administrative authorities. That is why its characteristic manifestation and most decisive test is disagreement with and dissent from authority. It is a space to which only other scholars may be admitted, and to them alone is one accountable. Second, little attention is given to the ways in which economic pressures and peer pressures limit one's freedom of inquiry and publication. For example, funds may be supplied for one kind of research but not another, or a certain school of thought or a particular scholar's work may be politically labeled as reactionary or radical, thereby dismissing it from serious academic attention and refusing it a hearing in appropriate professional meetings. Third, the limits on academic freedom are procedural rather than substantive. Methods of teaching or inquiry are to be judged incompetent, not the results of those methods; it is a violation of the ethics of the profession, not of the good of the human person, that limits academic freedom.

These observations are not made by way of criticism of the prevailing view of academic freedom. They are intended, rather, to highlight salient aspects of the view. It is also important to note what the prevailing professional view of academic freedom fails to consider. Academic freedom has at least three subjects,[22] not one, three claimants to the freedom called academic. The first subject or claimant is the academy itself, or in our North American context, a college or university.[23] This claim to freedom on the part of the academy is often referred to as a claim to *institutional autonomy*. Established by law and endowed with the authority to carry out specific tasks in keeping with its own stated mission, the academic institution as a whole claims the right to pursue its goals and exercise its authority without undue interference from any other agency external to itself. The word *undue* is a key word in that claim, for no academic institution does or can totally eschew external oversight and accountability. No academic institution would reasonably claim a right to exist for its own sake, but would defend its autonomy as essential for its service to the common good.[24]

The second subject or claimant of the freedom called academic is the individual faculty member, the person who is employed by the institution to carry out the tasks of teaching and research. It is important to note both that the institutional existence of the academy is made possible by political and/or ecclesiastical authorities external to itself, and that it is this social institutionalization of the college or university—with its legally established authority and immunity from external coercion—that provides a social space for the scholar's inquiry in the first place. It is the autonomy of the institution in which the scholar's freedom participates;

this institutional autonomy is the primary protection of the scholar's own continuing academic freedom.

The third subject of academic freedom is the student, the person who enrolls in the college or university in pursuit of knowledge and/or professional training and accreditation. It is true that, once accepted into the academy, students find themselves subjected to all kinds of restrictions and responsibilities. They are rightly expected to execute a variety of mandatory assignments and to meet certain performance standards in order to maintain their place in the academy and realize their goals. Nevertheless, if education is something different than mere indoctrination, there is a freedom appropriate to the student as student, and so properly called academic, which students advance as an immunity claim to noninterference in the choice of truths and values they claim as their own. This claim, made upon both the institution and the faculty, sets limits upon what both institution and faculty may require of the student. Neither may simply use the student for purposes of its own.[25]

Each of these three subjects, then—not just the faculty member—claims a right to academic freedom. Each subject claims the right in relation to both the subject's place in the larger society and to each one's peculiar role in the institution. As a right to act in specific ways without interference from external and internal authorities, academic freedom is undoubtedly a *negative* right, an immunity claim to noninterference as the subject seeks to pursue and fulfill a particular role in society and the institution. Surely an essential aspect of this right is the freedom to disagree with and dissent from the theoretical and practical views of all those who hold authority in or over the academy without fear of reprisal by those authorities.

Yet it is also certain that the different subjects of the right of academic freedom will have to define the content and the extent of their right with regard to the rights of the other subjects. The continued protection and realization of this right will be dependent in part on whether and how each of the subjects respects and supports the rights of the partners to academic freedom. That is to say, it is already the case that academic freedom entails not only a personal claim to noninterference, a negative right, but also the acceptance of a set of duties and responsibilities toward others. In this sense, one is ethically, if not legally, accountable to more than one's academic colleagues.

Academic freedom, then, is as much—if not more—the acceptance of a set of social relationships and obligations as it is the enjoyment of a right. This point is not adequately emphasized, to say the least, in professional views of the matter. It is a question of more than minor moment, then, whether the two limits on academic freedom, acknowledged in Lovejoy's definition above, adequately take account of this complex set of social relationships and obligations. It is also a crucial question whether the ways in which the academic freedom of institutions and faculty are socially embodied and protected give adequate scope for the effective exercise of their obligations to others that are corollaries of the right of academic freedom.[26]

LOVE, FREEDOM AND OBLIGATION: A CATHOLIC VIEW

To anyone even moderately familiar with the sacred Scriptures of the Hebrew and Christian religious traditions, it is evident that neighbor-concern is a central ethical feature in these religious faiths. What may not be so evident is the frequent incongruity of the biblical concern for the neighbor with the American cultural emphasis on individual rights understood as immunity claims to noninterference in the pursuit of one's own goals and interests.[27]

From the earliest pages of the book of Genesis, where the question of Cain, "Am I my brother's keeper?" (Gen. 4.10), has continued to ring through history, to the closing pages of the Gospel according to John where Jesus' new commandment, "Love one another as I have loved you," (John 15.12), encapsulates all of Christian morality, the focus on loving concern for one's neighbor is biblically unmistakable.[28] There simply is no authentic biblical faith that does not include neighbor-concern as a primary element. This simple truth has received its clearest and most forceful expression for Christian faith in the first Johannine epistle. "Anyone who says, 'I love God,' and hates his brother, is a liar, since a man who does not love the brother he can see cannot love God, whom he has never seen. So this is the commandment he has given us, that anyone who loves God must also love his brother." (1 John 4.20–21)

A closer scrutiny of the biblical texts reveals some distinctive features of the concern one is to have for the neighbor. It is a concern that centers in the Old Testament on the poor and the dispossessed; widows, orphans and aliens in the land are the exemplary objects of neighbor-concern. In the New Testament writings, the poor and the weak remain a central focus of concern, but neighbor-love finds its exemplary instance in love for one's enemies, for those who revile, persecute, rob and strike you (Matt. 5.38–48; Luke 6.27–35). Paul's letters are replete with examples of neighbor-concern, which include monetary help to the less fortunate (2 Cor. 8.1–15), a deliberate limiting of one's own freedom to avoid scandalizing the weaker neighbor (Rom. 14.1–23), and letting oneself be wronged or cheated rather than taking one's neighbor to court (1 Cor. 6.7–8).

What may be the most striking difference between the biblical emphasis on loving the neighbor and the contemporary American concern with claiming and insuring individual rights is the insistence, especially in the New Testament, that the followers of Jesus are not to think of themselves (Rom. 15.1–8) but are to become servants to their neighbors. They are not to be concerned with gaining or protecting their own rights but with meeting the needs of the neighbor and avoiding harm to the neighbor. "Love is the one thing that cannot hurt your neighbor; that is why it is the answer to every one of the commandments" (Rom. 13.10).

This all too brief sampling of the New Testament emphasis on neighbor-concern can be concluded by reference to the judgment parables in the Gospels according to Matthew and Luke. While service to one's neighbor does not exhaust the moral existence of the Christian believer, it does appear to be the most significant touchstone in deciding our final destiny. The rich man ignored the poor man Lazarus who lay at his gate covered with sores, and reaped, as his reward, eternal torment in Hades. (Luke 16.19–31). Those who fed the hungry, sheltered the homeless, clothed the naked, are welcomed into the kingdom of the Father, while those who neglected to come to the help of the needy neighbor are cast forth into eternal punishment. (Matt. 25.31–46). Seen in this light, neighbor-concern is not a gratuitous moral responsibility to be met when rights have been secured and justice satisfied, but a primary and serious moral obligation. Indeed, so basic is neighbor-concern to Christian life that the Epistle of James, reflecting the emphasis of the Hebrew Scriptures as well, can say quite simply, "Pure, unspoiled religion, in the eyes of God our Father, is this: coming to the help of orphans and widows, when they need it, and keeping oneself uncontaminated by the world" (James 1.27).

While this emphasis on concern for one's neighbor is beyond any serious dispute as a fundamental moral obligation of Christian life, the characteristics of neighbor-love are not equally uncontroversial or so readily acknowledged. One characteristic of such love is particularly problematic and especially relevant to the issue of freedom and dissent in the Church and so in church-related colleges and universities. This characteristic goes by the traditional name of *fraternal correction,* a correction that applies to errors by one's fellow human beings in matters of both doctrine and morality, or to both matters of what one teaches and how one behaves.

Christian love is clearly portrayed in the New Testament as both forgiving and servile, in the sense that it is a love that bears no grudges, harbors no resentments, and seeks to serve others without seeking reciprocity. It is nowhere portrayed, however, as being obsequious or without conviction. The brother or sister in the faith is to be corrected (Matt. 18.15–18), and even excommunicated, if that is judged to be necessary for his or her own good and the good of the community (1 Cor. 5.1–13; 2 Cor. 2.5–11, 13:3; 1 Thess 5.14–16; 2 Thess 3.10–15; Titus 1.10–14; 2 John 1.10–11; 3 John 1.9–11). Following the example of Jesus in his dealings with both Jewish and Roman authorities, Christian neighbor-love is never depicted as being weak and indecisive, and still less as obsequious or blind in its obedience to authority. It is rather strong, even unyielding, in its convictions and purpose, but never simply rebellious in principle, coercive in intent, or violent in practice.[29]

SIMILARITIES AND DIFFERENCES

For the correction of the neighbor in love to be a practical reality, however, and not merely fault-finding–or, worse, an exercise in the imposition of a stronger will upon a weaker one—three objective social conditions must be met, none of which are present in American society as a whole or in the vast majority of academic institutions in that society.[30] The first condition is that there must exist a community of shared faith and moral conviction, a community that also confesses that unity of faith and moral conviction to be a fundamental and normatively binding element of its identity. The second condition is the existence of some normative standard of truth and goodness to which individuals or the community can appeal as a basis for the corrective judgment. The third condition is a recognizable and acknowledged person or office to serve as a judge of these appeals on the basis of the normative standard.

The necessity and the importance of negative rights, and especially of the right to dissent, in American society—as also in the academic institutions of that society—are based in large measure upon the absence of these three conditions. It is because, as American citizens, we do not have a shared faith and shared moral convictions, no commonly accepted normative standard to which to appeal our differences in matters of truth and goodness, and so no judge to whom an appeal for a judgment of normative truth may be made, that the individual citizen is rightly left free to accept as true and good whatever commends itself to his or her own individual judgment.

The right to dissent, then, is exactly that, a right, in the sense of being an immunity from any legally established social coercion to think or judge in any particular way about what is true and good. The institutionalized right to dissent—most especially to dissent from the views and judgments of those in positions of power and authority—is, therefore, the requisite and indispensable social condition for any kind of political and social freedom for individuals and for minority groups. For freedom to be real in society, the right to dissent must be institutionalized in some way that effectively protects and promotes it.

The aim of the right to dissent, as institutionalized and given substantive form in the Bill of Rights of the Constitution of the United States, may be simply expressed as a freedom *from*, specifically from coercion in regard to what one holds to be true and good. It is a right acknowledged as due to individual citizens by virtue of their humanity, with no guarantee or expectation that truth and goodness will be achieved, or even sought, by individuals or by the community as a whole. And because there is in the American society as a whole no normative standard of truth and goodness by which any opinions, dissenting or otherwise, can be judged to be true or false, good or evil, no opinion can be grounds for dismissal from the body politic, not even the opinion that others should be denied the right to dissent.

Finally, because the highest political authority in the land, the Supreme Court of the United States, judges the compatibility of laws and procedures with the Constitution and *not* with what is either true or good by some transcendent standard, dissent in the political and social arenas does not necessarily cause the individual or a group to face a conflict of conscience or a clash of ethical loyalties. The pronouncements of the Supreme Court, while *legally* binding, are not *morally* binding as such on either our opinions or our behavior. Nor does our dissent from such pronouncements constitute us as either heretics or traitors. There is, to be sure, a transcendent ground for this right of the individual in political society to dissent from the established wisdom of the society.[31] The followers of Jesus are rightly ardent defenders and protectors of the right to dissent in civil society. But even without such a transcendent grounding, the right is sufficiently intelligible and pragmatically defensible.

Within the Church community itself, however, the case is very different. The Church community is, by its very constitution, a community of shared faith and moral conviction. It does have a normative standard of truth and goodness to which its members commonly appeal. Members of the community of faith are bound together in communion because they do not want or deem it right to think and act as their individual fancies, desires, or even their untutored use of reason[32] might dictate. They have willingly chosen to follow the Way, the Truth and the Life that is the Lord Jesus Christ. The freedom they seek in the Church is not primarily a freedom *from* but a freedom *for* truth and goodness. The requisite condition of this freedom, they have discovered, is not the right to dissent but faith and the obedience of faith. In the Roman Catholic communion, this obedience of faith includes free submission to the authentic teaching of the magisterium of the church.[33]

The aim, then, of Christian freedom, which does have its appropriate modes of free speech and diverse opinion, is not simply freedom from coercion. It is the freedom to know and live the truth as revealed in the community of the faithful by the Holy Spirit under the guidance of the magisterium. The truth that is faith is not the possession of the solitary individual, but of the church in which the individual shares. The individual may contribute to the understanding and development of the faith of the church by faithful living as well as by theological scholarship.

Because the community of faith does have a normative standard by which to judge claims about truth and goodness, heresy is always a real possibility. One may, indeed, cut oneself off from the communion of faith by holding to a different gospel. Christian love requires the community in such cases to make a judgment of error in order both to protect the unity of the community and to summon the straying member back to the path of truth. Such correction is not an infringement upon freedom but an obligation and service required of neighbor-love.

Finally, for one rooted in the Christian moral tradition, dissenting opinions voiced in the community of faith on matters of faith and morals do create a conflict of conscience. This conflict does not arise simply because someone or some group in the community has an opinion about a particular matter different than some authoritative pronouncement urges on us. Nor is the conflict of conscience even a matter of being convinced that one's personal moral duty lies elsewhere in a specific instance than where ecclesial authority proclaims it to lie. The conflicted conscience arises in the Christian experience when the demands of love come into apparent conflict in one's life. This conflict appears when love seems to require loyalty both to authority and to a contrary truth or course of action heralded by the dissenting voices. In such a situation, the loyal Christian is faced, not with a conflict between his or her own rights and the rights of others, but with a conflict of obligations demanded of him or her by one's love and loyalty to the Lord Jesus

Christ and to the service of God's people.[34]

In the context of a community of shared faith and moral conviction, therefore, theological dissent is not properly understood simply as the manifestation of an individual's right to freedom of opinion and expression. Theological dissent, if it is to be justified—i.e., seen as right—at all, is rather to be understood as a serious obligation and needed service of love, a prophetic burden as it were. For once the dissent has been spoken, it summons the entire community of faith to reform its doctrine and its life to accord more faithfully to the normative standard of truth and goodness, God's will, to which it appeals. Consequently, theological dissent within the community of faith can be expected to be a much less frequent reality than dissent in civil society,[35] and it is properly limited in ways that political or social dissent in the civil community is not, cannot and should not be limited. Nor can all interventions of ecclesiastical authority in response to dissenting voices be judged simply to be infringements upon either the personal or academic freedom of the theologian.[36]

Given the differences we have just detailed in the nature of the civil and ecclesial communities and in their understandings of freedom, rights and obligations, it is not at all surprising that each community has had different, perhaps even antithetical, concerns and interests in structuring its common life and finding social space for the realization of its values.[37] The American secular tradition, with its roots in classical liberalism,[38] has been largely concerned with how to institutionalize and protect the individual's freedom from various forms of political and ecclesiastical coercion. Rightly suspicious of the tendency of all social authority to overreach itself at the expense of the individual, the American tradition has chiefly concentrated on developing ways to limit that authority without rendering it altogether ineffective, and on establishing socially the structures and processes that would make, in regard to our present topic, academic freedom for the college or university and for its faculty and students a reality, not merely an ideal or ethical obligation to which individuals ought to aspire.

The two limits upon academic freedom mentioned earlier in Lovejoy's definition must be understood, therefore, as formal statements of the essential structural components of academic freedom that also try to provide for a measure of academic accountability. Specifically, such university mechanisms as periodic peer review, promotion and tenure, grievance procedures, faculty control of the curriculum, and external peer evaluations are designed to protect and promote academic freedom, as are the various rights, grievance procedures and judicial processes upon which students may call. Such measures are quite simply ways to institutionalize academic freedom in the interest of making it real and effective. Like all human efforts, these mechanisms and processes are imperfect and involve certain tradeoffs, but on the whole they have been found to effect what they were designed to effect: the freedom of faculty members in their teaching and research pursuits from certain kinds of external and internal coercion.[39]

The concern of the Roman Catholic church, however, in structuring and regulating its internal life and its external relations to the institutions of the societies in which it lives, has not been primarily to structure a space for individual freedom. Insofar as it has been concerned with freedom at all, it has been the freedom of the Church to be the Church. Consequently, the institutional autonomy of the Church itself has been the chief focus of concern,[40] as well as the freedom of its official agents—pope, bishops, clergy—over against political authority. In regard to its internal life, it has been more attentive to ways to institutionalize obligations and to provide space for the exercise of authority in those areas it judges to fall under ecclesiastical jurisdiction.

Toward this latter end, it has established, or tried to establish, juridical mechanisms whereby obligations are defined, lines of accountability from the bottom to the top of the social order are clear, and the exercise of ecclesiastical authority can be effective. Less suspicious of the likely abuses of ecclesial authority than either the Protestant or secular traditions, most likely for theological reasons,[41] the Roman Catholic faith tradition has acknowledged the legitimate freedom of individuals within the church, including the legitimate academic freedom of the theologian,[42] but has done little to give that freedom effective institutional ways to realize itself.[43]

The failure of the church to address the question of how to institutionalize freedom as it pertains to the academic life is vividly illustrated if one reads Pope John Paul II's "Apostolic Constitution on Catholic Universities," *Ex Corde Ecclesiae,*[44] or the "Instruction on the Ecclesial Vocation of the Theologian," issued by the Congregation for the Doctrine of the Faith.[45] A careful reading of *Ex Corde Ecclesiae* discovers exactly ten references to any kind of freedom, or 13 if three references to creativity in the university are counted as implying freedom.[46] Four of the remaining ten references are merely rhetorical flourishes.[47] Two are explicitly concerned with academic freedom in relation to civil society.[48] One is concerned with freedom of conscience, especially that of non-Catholic members of the university community. The other three simply assert the right to academic freedom with the admonition that such freedom is limited by the rights of individual persons and the community, and is further constrained by truth and the common good.[49]

A similar picture appears in the "Instruction." There one can find 15 references of one kind or another to freedom. Eight of those references are, in one form or another, to the truth that sets us free, i.e., the truth that is Jesus and the deeper freedom his salvation has brought to humanity.[50] Two are references to the freedom of inquiry and research proper to the theologian, but in both cases the limits on freedom are the major concern.[51] The other five references are to views of freedom that are declared to be false. For example, an ideology of philosophical liberalism, a right to dissent, the freedom of the act of faith as grounding a right to dissent, a principle of free examination, and a charge that rights are violated when church procedures are inadequate, are all mentioned only to be refuted.[52]

On the other hand, both documents are simply replete with moral exhortations and ethical claims about what universities should be and how theologians should behave. Above all, the rights of authority, not only to oversee the work of the university and the theologian, but also to intervene in order to ensure the appropriateness and correctness of these labors, are repeatedly stressed. The juridical mechanisms by which the social space for authority's actions can be effectively secured are spelled out by repeated references to the Code of Canon Law and other Roman documents.[53] Nothing of a similar nature is to be found concerning ways in which the social space required for academic freedom is to be effectively realized.

CONCLUSIONS

Whatever judgments one might make about the shortcomings of an institution structured in accord with liberal principles,[54] our concern here is with the adequacy or inadequacy of the official Roman Catholic understanding and practice of academic freedom. The judgment must be that not only is that understanding seriously inadequate, but in practice it also results in serious injustices to human persons. It is, quite simply, ethically flawed.

That judgment is a harsh one and is not wholly substantiated simply by pointing out the failure of official church documents to attend sufficiently to the effective institutionalization of the academic freedom it professes to esteem, albeit that is a serious shortcoming. By way of conclusion, then, I wish to offer a few additional considerations centered around the principle of *subsidiarity*.

The principle of subsidiarity is a fundamental, widely recognized principle of Catholic social thought, used originally by Pope Leo XIII in an implicit fashion to indicate the ethical limits upon the state's interventions in the economic order and to support the right of workers to unionize.[55] Taken up explicitly by John XXIII to urge a broader role for the state in regulating increasingly complex and interdependent human relationships,[56] it was also used by the American Catholic bishops in their two best known pastoral letters in the 1980s to argue for the creation of an international political authority and for a new American experiment in democracy.[57] The principle itself was clearly articulated by Pius XI as follows:

> ... it is a fundamental principle of social philosophy, fixed and unchangeable, that one should not withdraw from individuals and commit to the community what they can accomplish by their own enterprise and industry. So, too, it is an injustice and at the same time a grave evil and a disturbance of right order, to transfer to the larger and higher collectivity functions which can be performed and provided for by lesser and subordinate bodies. Inasmuch as every social activity should, by its very nature, prove a help to members of the body social, it should never destroy or absorb them.[58]

While there is some argument whether and to what extent the principle is appropriately applied to the life of the church itself, it is hard to see on what possible grounds its application to the life of the college or university in relation to the church can be denied or limited. If it is a fixed and unchangeable principle of social life, as the popes have taught, rooted in the nature of the human person and essential to the protection of human dignity and rights, on what possible grounds can it be refused a regulatory role in the life of the church and the university? The authority of the magisterium, like all authority derived from Jesus, is to be a service to—not a domination of—human persons, an ethical claim that the principle of subsidiarity clearly articulates. If authority as exercised in and by the church cannot meet the standard laid down by this fundamental principle of its own social philosophy, it surely cannot meet the more stringent test of Jesus' words and example.

Furthermore, there is no reason to think, given the centuries of experience we have had, that the authority of the church is any less capable of being misused and abused, of transgressing its limits and infringing upon the freedom and rights of individuals and groups in and outside the church. Authority in the church is as rightly constrained by ethical limits as any other legitimate authority exercised by human beings. For that constraint to be effective in practice, as moral truth requires it to be, institutional protection of the rights and freedoms of individuals is essential. It is, then, not the teaching of documents like *Ex Corde Ecclesiae* or the "Instruction on the Ecclesial Vocation of the Theologian" that is particularly a problem, but the institutional practice of authority envisaged in these documents that raises serious objections.

If the academic freedom of the theologian is to be real, then the theologian, no more and no less than any other faculty member, is owed socially institutionalized protection from both political and ecclesiastical authority. Since the effective institutionalization of academic freedom requires the protection both of institutional autonomy and of the rights and processes accorded faculty and students within the institution, the principle of subsidiarity inescapably requires that juridical limits be placed upon external authority's practical ability to constrain either the institution's right to govern itself as it judges proper or the teaching and research of individual faculty members. Failure in this regard is the practical negation of the principle of subsidiarity and of the right of academic freedom.

Such a position neither denies nor renders ineffective the ecclesial magisterium's responsibility for overseeing the faith and moral practice of the church, nor its right and obligation to intervene, inquire into, and even censure a theologian's work or a Catholic institution's practice when teaching or practice contrary to the faith must be addressed.

The magisterial office has available to it a variety of social spaces in which to exercise its responsibilities. Few administrative officials in Catholic institutions and few theologians would refuse an invitation to discuss with their bishops opinions or practices about which their bishops were concerned. The pulpits of every church in the diocese are open to the bishop of the diocese, as are the pages of the diocesean newspaper and the parish bulletin. Gaining access to the secular press and other public media, when necessary, is not a particularly difficult matter for bishops in liberal societies. There simply is no shortage of forums in which public correction or censure of, and ecclesial disassociation from, a Catholic institution's or a particular theologian's spoken or written views can be effected.

The kind of magisterial control over academic institutions called for in official church documents, and the kind of institutional control over theologians also advocated in these documents, are neither warranted as a service to the church, the academic institution or the theologian, nor required for the proper exercise of magisterial responsibility. They are simply unwarranted infringements upon the legitimate, albeit relative autonomy of academic institutions and faculty members. In the language of the principle of subsidiarity, magisterial control over colleges and universities, and over any or all of their faculty, is not a help to the body social, but rather tends to destroy them or absorb them into purposes alien to their mission.

Finally, a word should be added about the responsibility of the institutions and the faculty members who are the subjects of academic freedom. All academic disciplines rely upon and require, for their authentic development, the personal integrity of those who study and profess them. The pursuit of knowledge and truth, as well as its communication and systematic extension, is a moral

enterprise as much as it is an intellectual one. This is
the case for every teacher and scholar no more and no
less than it is for the theologian.

Church authority is, therefore, quite correct to stress
the important moral requirements attendant upon the
work of Catholic universities and the work of the
theologian. For it is the case that the competent Catholic
theologian does have stringent moral obligations of loyal
respect for magisterial teaching and of concern for the
unity and well-being of the ecclesial community. It is
also the case that a college or university that calls itself
Catholic has an obligation to its constituents and its
public to attempt to reflect that identity in its policies
and practices both internally in the conduct of it own
affairs and externally in its relations to other social bodies.

But it is also the case that, because the academic life
is a moral enterprise, it requires freedom of inquiry,
communication, publication and discussion as essential
conditions of its exercise. It is why that freedom must
be protected in all its dimensions against directly coercive reprisals from all authority external to the academy.
When the work of the academy ceases to be done as a
result of the free, moral commitment of its members,
education ceases and indoctrination begins.[59]

I know of no competent Catholic theologian who denies the right and the obligation of the magisterium to
inquire into, challenge, censure, or even condemn the
theological views expressed in written or spoken form
by any Catholic theologian who puts them forth as
authentic expressions of the faith of the church. As
Rahner's view, cited earlier, puts it, there is no violation of personal right or academic freedom necessarily
involved in such cases. Violation of right occurs, if it
occurs at all, when the magisterium acts in this way
without observing the processes of justice due in fairness to anyone being accused of error or wrongdoing,[60]
or when it threatens or carries out a directly punitive
authority in an arena in which it has no ethical right.

It has often been argued that Catholic University's

special juridical relationship to the Vatican made the case of Professor Charles E. Curran different, and that the academic freedom of the theologian itself must be thought of in a different way than the freedom appropriate to professors of other disciplines. Legally, the first point is well taken, as the judgment rendered by the court in the Curran case was at pains to stress.[61] Ethically, however, one would insist in such circumstances, as a minimum requirement of justice, that these differences, as the institution sees them, be spelled out in writing and the processes by which faculty are protected from arbitrary decisions of authority be laid down in as much written detail as possible.[62]

I do not claim here that there is a necessary and *de facto* injustice perpetrated whenever a college or university chooses to surrender its institutional autonomy to an external authority. Avery Dulles has pointed out that working under a canonical mandate does not seem to have restricted the freedom of several outstanding theologians.[63] But, of course, it is quite possible to live within a system marred by structural injustice without oneself being a victim of injustice. That fortuity does not exempt one from recognizing and acting against the structural injustice. When institutional autonomy is surrendered by a college or university, justice would seem to require that the faculty who teach there, the students who study there, and the public who sustain the social context of the institution be made explicitly aware of the fact, and that claims to institutional autonomy and academic freedom be eliminated from the institution's self-description and self-promotion.

2. Academic Freedom: American and European Contexts

Raymond F. Collins

How true it is that we are often unable to see the forest because of the trees. In the midst of a situation, we can be so caught up with details that we are unable to get a perspective on the whole.

In contrast, life abroad frequently provides a good perspective from which to view things at home. Life abroad often enables a person to develop a vision of one's life at home that life at home is unable to provide. It is from my perspective as an American abroad and from my personal experience as an American abroad that I dare to make a modest contribution to this collection of essays on "Academic Freedom."

A Few Vignettes

The stories of biblicists like David Friedrich Strauss (1808–1874) and Julius Wellhausen (1844–1918) are well known. Strauss's 1835 publication of *The Life of Jesus* resulted in the loss of his post at Tübingen. Called to Zurich as professor of theology at the age of 31, Strauss was pensioned off before the official inauguration of his professorship. His premature retirement was the result of opposition from conservative believers.

Wellhausen's 1879 publication of *The History of Israel* led to his resignation from the theological faculty at Greifswald and his assumption of a position—in Semitic languages—at the University of Halle. This, incidentally, allowed him to further his historical inquiry into the New Testament. Wellhausen's story brings to mind the somewhat later history of Père Lagrange whose espousal of theories on the origin of the Pentateuch, similar to those advanced by Wellhausen, raised such strong opposition on the part of Roman Catholic authorities that Lagrange abandoned his study of the Hebrew Scriptures. Thereafter he devoted himself exclusively to the study of the New Testament, a field in which he made important contributions in the early decades of this century.

Closer to Home

I could move the story somewhat closer to home by using the Catholic University of Leuven as the locale. Established as Studium Generale by Pope Martin V's papal bull in 1425, the Faculty of Theology was inaugurated as the new university's fourth faculty in 1432, taking its place alongside the older faculties of arts, law and medicine. Closed under the French Republic in 1797, the University of Leuven reopened as a state university in 1816. While Belgium was in the process of becoming a new nation (1830), the bishops of Belgium began a series of meetings that led to the formation of a Catholic University in Mechlin in 1834. Moved to Leuven (Louvain) in 1835, it replaced the secular university with one that continued the former tradition of a University of Leuven under Catholic auspices.

The Catholic University of Leuven's character as both *Catholic* and *university* was to inspire John Henry Newman's idea of a university and plant a seminal idea in the minds of those who were responsible for the establishment of the Catholic University of America. Despite its pronounced character as both Catholic and university—reemphasized in the university's Mission Statement of 16 March 1990—the history of Leuven's university for the past 150 years is full of stories of tension between various ecclesiastical authorities, especially Roman authorities, and biblical researchers working within the *alma mater*. Let me give two examples, one from the early part of this century dealing with Old Testament research, the other a more recent example dealing with the New Testament.

Albin van Hoonacker (1857–1933), at one time a consultant to the Pontifical Biblical Commission, saw his work on the minor prophets subject to animadversions by the Congregation of the Index. Van Hoonacker's career survived, and indeed continued to flourish, only because of Cardinal Desiré Mercier. At the time, Mercier was van Hoonacker's ordinary, the archbishop of Mechlin and the grand chancellor of the University of Leuven. Mercier not only lent his personal support to van Hoonacker, but also intervened on the latter's behalf in correspondence with Cardinal Merry del Val[1] and the Pope himself.

Almost a half century later, at the time of the discussions leading to the drafting and promulgation of *Dei Verbum*, Vatican Council II's dogmatic Constitution on Divine Revelation, a group of cardinals, including Ruffini and McIntyre,[2] cited a small work on the Lukan Infancy narrative by Leuven's Frans Neirynck as an example of a departure from the principles of Catholic hermeneutics.[3] Their complaint was lodged at approximately the same time that Professors Lyonnet and Zerwick were being stopped from teaching biblical exegesis at Rome's Pontifical Biblical Institute.[4]

At Home and Abroad

The vignettes could be multiplied. The few examples I have cited merely illustrate how ecclesiastical authorities—Roman Catholic authorities as well as those of other Christian churches—have impinged upon the exercise of research and publication in the limited field of biblical studies. The examples also show that conflict between academic inquiry and ecclesiastical authority is not unknown in European academic circles. The struggle for academic freedom, specifically with regard to theological inquiry, is hardly confined to North America and its institutions of higher learning.

For European theologians the issue of academic freedom is not merely a matter for theoretical reflection. Issues of academic freedom occupy a major place in the institutional memory. They continue to engage the minds and energies of European theologians. As a matter of fact, at approximately the same time that the Catholic University of Leuven was in the process of drafting its mission statement, articulating a vision of the contemporary University as both Catholic and university, its bioethicists and university administrators were party to discussions with Roman authorities on the matter of *in vitro* fertilization and other beginning-of-life issues. In addition, a significant percentage of the professors of the Faculty of Theology were lending their support to the Cologne Declaration by cosigning that document.

AN OUTSIDER'S VIEW

Recognizing that a European perspective on academic freedom is a topic much too vast to be adequately sketched, let alone thoroughly treated, within a few short pages, let me offer but a few thoughts on academic freedom from the perspective of an American abroad. Assuming the stance of outsider, I shall try to get a fix on the *gestalt* of academic freedom in North America and compare that with an experience of academic freedom in a European context.

Immediately three features of the pursuit of academic freedom in the North American context strike the European most forcefully. These are its democratic inspiration, the role of law and its frontier spirit.

Democratic Inspiration

First, its democratic inspiration. The Declaration of Independence, with its declaration of inalienable rights to "life, liberty and the pursuit of happiness" (4 July 1776), preceded the French Republic's Declaration of the Rights of Man and of the Citizen (5 October 1789) by more than 13 years. The second article of this document spoke of man's inalienable right to "liberty, property, security, and resistance to oppression."

While both the Declaration of Independence and the Declaration of the Rights of Man were essentially concerned with political rights, the language of the Declaration of Independence is more comprehensive. Of particular importance for the history of higher education and the matter of academic freedom is the fact that most American colleges and universities were established after the writing of the Declaration of Independence. Only nine colleges had been founded before this. In contrast, the great universities of Europe had already been established by the time of the Declaration of the Rights of Man. For example, my own university, the Catholic University of Leuven, was second only to Paris in prestige and numbers of students some two centuries before the Declaration of Independence and the Declaration of the Rights of Man were proclaimed. The older European universities continue to provide the idea of a university for the more recent university foundations. The older universities are not so much a norm or standard as they are a model or paradigm[5] for the newer universities on the European continent.

The Declaration of the Rights of Man has not, moreover, imbued the European ethos with its spirit as thoroughly as the Declaration of Independence has shaped the American ethos and the institutions that have developed within it. To be overly simplistic, one might say that the American university was born in a climate of political freedom—one in which political freedom was in the forefront of the common consciousness—whereas the classic European university came into being before a consensus on the importance of political freedom had been achieved. As a result, academic freedom in the American university appears, to an outside observer, to be the child of political freedom. Academic freedom in the European setting is clearly *not* such a child.

As a function of the democratic institution and reflecting its democratic spirit, American academic freedom is freedom from outside interference—that is, freedom from external coercion, especially political and governmental interference in academic research. The denial of academic freedom is simply "un-American." It is inconsistent with American standards of fair play.

Another aspect of academic freedom in North America is the support which it receives from other democratic institutions, those that are political by nature. Academic freedom is supported by the right to free assembly. Academic freedom appears to be a function of free speech. Confrontation, rallies and strikes are much in evidence when academic freedom is in danger of being curtailed or suspended.

Academic freedom is also bolstered by a free press. When academic freedom is threatened, one can count on appeals to the press with open letters, paid advertisements, press conferences and the like. By and large, in the European experience academic freedom is not so closely linked to the fabric of the national ethos as it is in the American experience.

The Role of Law

Secondly, the role of law and statute. It is difficult to assess the function of a legislative system in determining the national ethos and the values that motivate society. Nonetheless, one can say that a system of common law and its jurisprudence shapes a society and its values in a way different from those associated with the various European legal systems, particularly those dependent upon the Napoleonic code. A system of common law presumes that the law embodies the values of society and the responsible consensus of the people.

In some ways, the legal system of North America seems to be more pervasive than the various European systems. Americans are, by and large, more litigious than are Europeans. Law students in the University of Leuven, where the school of law is the third largest school of the university—after business and medicine—are struck by what can only appear to be the glut of lawyers in the United States. "The Agenda for Civil Justice Reform in America," a report from the President's Council on Competitiveness, indicates that the United States has 281 lawyers per 100,000 citizens. In contrast, Germany, where the standard of living, economic competitiveness and academic interests are every bit as high as they are in the United States, has but 111 lawyers per comparable segment of the population. England and Wales, whose system of common law preceded and inspired our own, has only 82 lawyers for each population of 100,000 persons.[6]

It is difficult to say whether the American character is more contentious than is that of other peoples, whether economic and related interests are the ultimate cause of American litigation, or whether it is our system or jurisprudence that spawns appeals to the courts. Regardless of the cause, academic matters are much more often subject to litigation in North America than they are in other countries. Litigation may take place under the jurisdiction of a university's internal statues, the contractual provisions between the members of the AAUP, for example, and a university, or the provisions of common civil law. At each of these levels, issues of academic freedom are more often the object of the litigation than they are in Europe. As one of my European colleges recently put it, recourse to the courts is much more a part of American culture than it is in Europe. It is, said this colleague, a cultural matter.

Norms of academic freedom are much more clearly defined and precisely spelled out in North America than they are in Europe. Violation of any of these norms is much more readily subject to judicial process in the United States. Academic freedom is a civil right, whose implications are spelled out in various statutes and whose violations are subject to due process and litigation procedures. Denial of academic freedom is, as has been said, not only unfair, it is also un-American.

Frontier Spirit

Thirdly, the frontier spirit of academic freedom in the United States. "Frontier spirit" may not be a proper epithet to be used in a description of academic freedom, but in the eyes of many a European the frontier spirit seems to qualify the American experience of academic freedom.

Under this rubric, I can cite the argumentative spirit that seems to characterize academic freedom in the United States. The typical American academician is much more ready to pick a fight in the name of academic freedom than is his or her European counterpart. Along these lines, there appears to be an American tendency to push academic freedom to the frontier, to push the parameters to their outermost limits. In the name of academic freedom, one should go as far as one can.

As part of the frontier experience, one can also point to what appears to be an occasional "Lone Ranger" aspect of academic freedom in the United States. To the European, the pursuit of academic freedom in America often appears to be a matter of pursuing one's individual rights, with comparatively little attention being paid to the ultimate foundation of those rights. The pursuit of academic freedom is a matter of pursuing one's rights as much as, or perhaps even more than, it is a matter of pursuing the truth.

As a result of this individualism, as well as the American tendency "to go the whole nine yards," great tolerance is accorded to various ideas and practices in the name of academic freedom. Many of these ideas and practices appear quite strange within a European setting.

Here and Now

To all this should be added the American fixation on the here and now. All that is good must happen immediately. Americans dare not leave until tomorrow what can be achieved today. Thus it appears to the European eye that the American pursuit of academic freedom is characterized by urgency and immediacy. Within the American pursuit of academic freedom, there lies a profound desire to bring issues to clear and immediate closure.

A EUROPEAN EXPERIENCE

It is difficult to write about the European experience of academic freedom because the experience varies so much from country to country, sometimes even from institution to institution within a single country, even one as small as Belgium. One could write about academic freedom in general or academic freedom in particular— that is, academic freedom and theological inquiry. Given this vast scope, I shall, as I have indicated, offer but a few reflections based on my experience rather than present the results of academic research.

One obvious result of my European academic experience is the realization that the context in which the issue of academic freedom is raised is quite different from the context in which it is raised in the United States. One can hardly say that the European idea of a university is totally different from the American idea, but there are significant differences.

Tradition, History and Memory

Some of the more important differences can be summed up under the related rubrics of history and tradition. The European university has a long memory. Theological conflicts are part of its institutional history. When one looks at the history of the Catholic University of Leuven, for example, one encounters the names of Baius and Jansenius. Leuven's condemnation of Luther and the censure of Lessius are part of its history. At various moments in history, members of Leuven's Faculty of Theology have been involved in censure—on both sides of the docket!

The long view of history and institutional participation in a relatively long segment of history brings an awareness that truth—and specifically theological truth—is not attained in a single moment. It is arrived at by means of ongoing inquiry, in the course of which partial realizations of the truth can and must be seen as partial attainments of truth and partial embodiments of error.

Academic Freedom

This brief reflection serves to introduce what well may be the two most important differences between the European experience and understanding of academic freedom and the American experience and understanding of this freedom. In the American experience, it is the freedom *from* that is most important, whereas in the European experience it is the freedom *for* that matters most. Admittedly, this is but a matter of emphasis. Nonetheless, the different emphasis provides a similar value with a different gestalt. In the American

experience, academic freedom is a matter of the academician's freedom *from* institutional constraints—be they
political, ecclesiastical or academic-institutional—while
teaching and doing research. In the European experience,
in contrast, academic freedom is essentially viewed as
freedom to seek *for* the truth.

A second and related feature that distinguishes the
European experience and understanding from the American is the value suggested, embodied and protected by
academic freedom. In the American experience, that value
is principally personal liberty and integrity; in the
European experience, the value is truth itself. Once again,
sharp and truly adequate distinctions ought not to be
made in this regard, but there is a manifest difference
between the American and European experiences of
academic freedom. To a large extent, the difference bears
upon the value at stake. On the one hand, it is personal
rights; on the other, it is the right of truth.

One might legitimately ask whether truth has any
rights. The question has been asked over and over again.
Merely raising the question brings painful memories to
the fore, especially for Western Christians. The horrors
of the Inquisition are but one expression of the excesses
to which an unbridled proclamation of the rights of truth
so easily leads. More recent Roman Catholic discussions
on religious freedom, happily brought to closure by Vatican Council II's Declaration on Religious Freedom,
bespoke the intolerance and destruction that were the
byproducts of a vision in which "error has no rights."

Few if any—one must always make exception for the
extreme rightist who occasionally makes his or her way
into the academic enterprise—European academicians
would justify these excesses today. Nonetheless, there
is something of a fascination for the truth, as a value
in itself, which continues to characterize the European
academic experience and the fashion in which it con-
ducts its theological inquiry.

Since rights belong to human beings rather than to
abstract realities such as "the truth," the discussion

ought not to be about the rights of truth. The discussion ought rather to focus upon peoples' right *to* the truth. When the discussion is so moved, one implicitly touches upon a philosophical difference that ultimately serves to distinguish the European experience of academic freedom from the American. This is a difference in philosophical anthropology.

A Personal Matter

It is the person who has the right to truth. But what—indeed, who—is the person? What do we understand by the "human person?" To continue with the broad strokes that have characterized this essay, the general understanding of the person within the United States emphasizes the uniqueness of the individual, whereas the typical European understanding focuses upon the individual in solidarity with others. Individuality is the hallmark of the person from the American perspective; sociality is *the* characteristic of the person from the European perspective. A modern *Louvaniste* cannot help but recall Professor Louis Janssens's significant reflections on the norm of morality, that is, the human person adequately considered in itself and its relationships.[7]

The social aspect of the human person, so emphasized in European philosophical discussion and embodied in a variety of social structures in the European social democracies, has its bearing upon the issue of academic freedom. In the European experience, people have the right to know the truth; in the American experience, individuals have a right to pursue the truth and to use it for their personal advantage. The European is wary lest the truth, once attained, become subservient to the self-serving interests of an individual or of a particular group—whether the group be made up of a relatively small number of individuals or defined by larger corporate or national interests.

An anecdote might illustrate this difference of approach. The endowed chair is a well-known feature of the American university. The system allows American universities to attract professors who would not otherwise be drawn to a particular university. Endowments also provide funding for research projects that would not otherwise be part of a university's endeavor. Indeed, a good number of endowments is a sign of the flourishing university in North America.

In some ways, the endowed chair even helps to undergird academic freedom as it provides professors and researchers with some measure of independence from university structures. The other side of the coin is, however, that endowments are frequently made in pursuit of relatively narrow corporate interests. The story of Stanford's Donald Kennedy is but a token of the less-than-ideal results of the American alliance between academia and government and/or business. In that case, monies "for scientific research" provided for a university yacht and other private perks.

Endowed chairs and buildings are, by and large, unknown in the University of Leuven. Recently the Faculty of Theology at the University of Leuven had occasion to weigh the establishment of an endowed chair for the Study of American Values. When the proposal was submitted to the *Bureau*, a body akin to a faculty senate but with much greater authority,[8] a good amount of hesitation was voiced. The cause of this hesitation had to do with the source of funding. Would the proposed chair be corporately funded? If so, to what extent would those who provided funding for the chair have a voice in the naming of the chairholder and/or the content of research and teaching conducted under the aegis of the chair?

Fortunately the issue was happily resolved, and the chair inaugurated. The discussion, however, points to a typical European caution. The pursuit of truth must not become subservient to limited interests.

No less indicative of this caution was the vigorous protest undertaken by various student groups at the University of Leuven when the University decided to grant an honorary degree to one of its own alumni, who, however, also happened to be the CEO of the Janssens Pharmaceutical Corporation.[9]

Europeans proclaim people's right to pursue the truth within an academic context, but they view that right as one that belongs to persons who are social by nature and who are convinced that the truth must be placed at the service of the broadest possible segment of humanity.

Here-and-now, Either-or and the Particular

In short, the European experience of how truth has been and is to be attained gives a different allure to academic freedom from that which Americans have come to know. Although these qualities have already been suggested, it might not be superfluous to underscore three qualities of the European pursuit for truth—within an academic setting, to be sure—which further distinguish it from its American counterpart and contribute to a distinctively European experience of academic freedom.

Here-and-now, either-or and a *focus upon the particular* pertain to the fabric of the American ethos and have their impact on academia and academic freedom. Little need be said about the American obsession with immediate results. "Tomorrow" comes with difficulty to American lips and seems not to fit within the American vision of things. The American's efforts, often not unmixed with pragmatic concerns, is characterized by urgency; in contrast, the European's pursuit of the truth is one that is more comfortable with the historical process. Within the European setting, academic freedom is a value that must be maintained so that, within the long course of history, truth may be achieved. Americans require the affirmation of academic freedom in the immediacy of the present hour.

By and large, Americans have a bipolar view of reality. Either-or is a characteristic way of thinking and acting. In matters academic, as in social relationships, the American is uneasy with compromise and the more-or-less. The American views another individual or another nation as either *for* or *against*. The American tends to think in absolutes. Judgments are made in terms of black or white rather than in terms of gray. Compromise and more-or-less agreement are foreign to the American way of thinking. This has its bearing upon the American experience of academic freedom insofar as the American is intolerant of truth mixed with error, whereas the European is more comfortable with the amalgam, confident that the truth will eventually win out. A longer memory contributes to comfort and confidence. Creative tension is part of the experience and a necessary component of the pursuit of the truth.

Finally, the American way of thinking and acting tends to focus upon the particular. Politically, Americans tend to be one-issue oriented. In matters academic and theological/ecclesiastical, Americans are easily inclined to focus on one issue—to the exclusion of a broader vision of reality! Once again it would be overly simplistic and indeed erroneous to say that the American has tunnel vision and the European a broad perspective, but there is some measure of truth in caricature. In the pursuit of truth, Americans focus on one aspect, whereas Europeans tend to interrelate the one to the many, the particular to the general.

Two examples, taken from the realms of theology and ecclesial practice, can but suggest the point. In my university, theology is still taught according to a classic model. The study of Scripture and historical theology, of systematics and ethics, of sacrament and ritual, of pastoral practice and church law is part of the program, even at the graduate level.[10] Students are expected to be conversant with the whole range of theology. Evaluation of students essentially consists of an appreciation of the work of an entire academic year, not of its component parts or credits. This approach contrasts sharply with the American experience, in which a theological student may be well versed in one theological discipline, but virtually ignorant of another.

An obvious example of the way in which Americans tend to isolate their experience—and their appreciation of values—is the present conflict between adherents to the pro-choice movement and those who are pro-life. The former see things in terms of a woman's choice, irrespective of the rights of her mate and those that might be attributed to a developing human life. On the other hand, the latter narrowly see matters from the perspective of the sanctity of fetal life. Some of the pro-lifers, Roman Catholics included, were not pleased by Cardinal Bernardin's use of the metaphor of the "seamless garment," by which he urged that the matter of the value and dignity of human life be considered in a broad perspective. The cardinal's critics complained that he had confused the issue by daring to associate the Christian appreciation of the right to life with anything other than the unborn baby's right to life.

It would be foolhardy to suggest that within the American experience there are not those who have a longer vision of things, who appreciate the complexity of reality, or who have a holistic approach to issues. Nor can I claim that the European academician never appreciates the urgency of certain issues, never proffers a yes-or-no answer, or never considers one issue in isolation from another. I would simply suggest that the European intellectual context typically provides the European thinker and his or her university with a matrix of thought that leads to a different experience of academic freedom, one in which other values and other ways of pursuing a similar value come to the fore.

Authorities and Academicians

As regards academic freedom and theological inquiry, there is yet one more significant difference between the European and American experiences of academic freedom. This has to do with the academic background of European ecclesiastical authorities, especially Roman Catholic authorities. To a much greater extent than is the case in the United States, Europe's Roman Catholic bishops have received advanced theological degrees and have personally participated in the academic enterprise. This creates a situation in which "theological dissent" is seen less as an affront to ecclesiastical authority than as a matter of theological discussion. One might suggest that European ecclesiastical authorities have more understanding of the process by means of which theological truth is attained than do their American counterparts.

Here, too, the long range of history, the sense of theological nuance and the danger of reducing one's vision to a single focal point have their roles to play in providing the European theologian with a context in which theological research is carried on within a perspective of academic freedom. In other words, there is a freedom to pursue theological truth that somehow transcends the boundaries of temporal and spatial limitation.

One should, moreover, not overlook the historical differences between the development of the church[11] in the United States and Canada and the history of the church in Europe. In Europe, local churches were developed before the modern states were configured.

These local churches had their own history and developed their own character before the Roman church became as centralized as it has tended to become in the past 125 years. The relative autonomy of these churches contributes, even now, to the creation of a context wherein theologians are relatively free to pursue their theological inquiry with freedom and responsibility.

In contrast with the relative autonomy of the European dioceses, the church in North America has tended to be more centralized. To a large extent, this is due to the fact that the church was developed under the aegis of the Congregation for the Propagation of the Faith. To an equally large extent, this is due to the fact that the North American church has been a minority church. The strength of a church under pressure tends to produce a common front. The need for a common front is not apparent in Europe; its history of theological diversity makes uniformity seem out of place and inconsistent with the nature of the pursuit of theological truth.

EPILOGUE

This "essay from abroad" is much too short and thus necessarily lacks the nuance that this matter deserves. Even as I have written, I have felt a strong need to qualify my remarks, develop the perspectives and add explanatory footnotes. Constraints of space preclude any consideration of the details. What is offered, then, is a quick glance at the forest of academic freedom, at the very high price of failing to look at the trees of individual experience.

3 • The Teaching Mission of the Church and Academic Freedom

Avery Dulles, S.J.

The question of academic freedom in Catholic universities has been much discussed in recent years, but as yet we seem to be far from achieving a consensus, even among Catholic specialists. I shall try to cast some light on the question by considering the role of the university and its religious education programs in relation to the magisterium, or teaching authority, of the Catholic church. What does it mean to say that the church teaches? Is the teaching of the church a synonym for that of the hierarchical magisterium? If so, what place remains for the teaching of parents, catechists, and theologians? Can university theologians, in the name of academic freedom, claim the right to teach in opposition to the pope and the bishops? And if not, can they be said to have academic freedom at all? In view of the complexity of these questions, I shall consider myself successful if I can manage to avoid further confusing an already confused discussion.

THE TEACHING MISSION OF THE CHURCH

Let me begin by attempting to elucidate what it means to speak of "the teaching mission of the church." What does the church teach, and how?

According to a widely prevalent theological convention, endorsed by the documents of Vatican Council II, Jesus Christ had a threefold office as prophet, priest and king. In his prophetic office he spoke to the world in the name of God. The term "prophet" in this context means one who speaks in the name of another—i.e., God. In Greek the verb *pro-phemi* means to speak on behalf of; a *pro-phetes* is a spokesperson. As prophet of God, Jesus announced the advent of the eschatological kingdom. But he did more than deliver a bare announcement. He also instructed his disciples in the mysteries of the kingdom. This authoritative instruction constitutes what we may call the prophetic teaching of Jesus. It is prophetic in the technical sense that Jesus spoke authoritatively as sent by the Father.

The church as a whole participates in the threefold office of Christ. As explained in Vatican II's Dogmatic Constitution, *Lumen gentium*, the church, as prophet, has the task of announcing the good news, or of evangelizing. As an authoritative witness, it continues to proclaim the good news given in Christ. But it does more than proclaim. It also has the task of offering precise and progressive instruction to its faithful so that they may to some extent understand the message they have received. This instruction may be called teaching.

Teaching may be attributed to the church as a whole, but it is actually carried out by particular persons. The popes and bishops have an indispensable role in the total process, but they are not the sole educators of the faithful in matters of religion. Parents, according to Vatican II, are the first educators of their children.[1] Every Christian believer, by virtue of baptism and confirmation, has a vocation to be a witness to the gospel, and those who are reflective and educated in their faith have the capacity and the responsibility to instruct others.

The church as a corporate body has the obligation to see to it that the faith is not corrupted or distorted in the process of transmission. For this reason certain controls are established. The entire process of transmission takes place under the supervision of the pope and the bishops, who are divinely appointed successors of the Apostles in maintaining the correct understanding of the Christian message. The bishops have among their principal duties those of personally preaching the faith and instructing their people through sermons and pastoral letters. Their most effective teaching is often done when they associate others with themselves in the teaching apostolate. Priests and deacons, who are ordained to preach and to teach, are closely associated with the bishops. So also are a multitude of religious educators and catechists, some of whom function in Catholic schools, others in parishes and nonacademic situations.

It is helpful, therefore, to distinguish two ways in which the church teaches—the official and the unofficial. It teaches officially through the pope and the bishops, who are by divine institution empowered to teach in the name of Christ. These officeholders speak in the name of the church, in the sense that their official positions are those of the church as a public institution. They have the right and duty to establish the doctrine of the church as such. Without an official teaching organ, the church would not be able to maintain a coherent body of teaching, and it would in that regard be deficient in carrying on the prophetic ministry of Christ. But the hierarchical officeholders are not the sole agents by whom the church teaches. It teaches unofficially by means of those of its faithful who have sufficient knowledge to be able to bring others to a certain understanding of the faith. Religious instruction on the elementary level is called catechesis; on higher levels it takes the form of advanced courses in Christian doctrine and theology. The entire process of Christian education takes place under the supervision of the hierarchical magisterium. To assure the proper continuity between official magisterial teaching and day-to-day religious education, some teachers of religion are given an office or commission from the hierarchy.

THEOLOGIANS AS TEACHERS IN THE CHURCH

All education in Christian doctrine involves a measure of reflective understanding of the Christian message and thus may be called, in some sense, theology. Theology has been defined in many ways, but it is difficult to improve on the phrase of Anselm, who spoke of "faith seeking understanding." Every believer who seeks to acquire or impart an understanding of the faith may be called, at least in a rudimentary way, a theologian or a teacher of theology.

In modern times, the term *theology* is usually restricted to scholarly reflection upon the faith by persons who have attained a high degree of competence, normally certified by advanced degrees or noteworthy publications. In their pondering of the faith, theologians normally deal with questions such as these: What are the precise meanings of the accepted statements of faith? What is the basis of such statements in the sources of revealed knowledge? How can the credibility of such statements be shown? What is their inner coherence and intelligibility in relation to the total Christian message? What relevance do they have for the human quest? What are the theoretical and practical consequences of the things that Christians believe, or should believe? The theologian seeks to answer such questions by drawing on all the sources of knowledge that might prove helpful, but the most basic reference point for theology is the faith itself, authoritatively set forth in normative documents.

In recent years there has been some debate about whether or not the theologian must be a believer. Normally theologians are believers, for there would be little point in attempting to explore the implications of a faith one did not accept. Furthermore, it may be doubted whether a nonbeliever could be a really competent theologian. One who simply looks at a religion from outside without sharing its beliefs, I would argue, will rarely be a good interpreter of the tenets and implications of that religion. We may conclude, then, that theology is a reflection upon faith from within the commitment of faith. Those who attempt a purely detached analysis may be engaged in some legitimate type of religious studies, but they generally remain at the surface level and fail to achieve the kind of penetration that is expected in theology.

What, then, must the theologian accept? To do Christian theology at all one has to acknowledge the existence of God, the fact of revelation, the centrality of Christ in God's saving plan, and the reliable transmission of the gospel through Scripture and the Church. In addition, Catholic theology is predicated upon the validity of the Catholic tradition and upon the guidance offered by the hierarchical magisterium. The Catholic theologian who wishes to remain a Catholic is bound to accept the definitive or irreformable doctrine of the magisterium and must be favorably disposed to accepting whatever the magisterium puts forth as obligatory doctrine.

There are limits, therefore, to the freedom of theology. Under pain of self-destruction, it is prevented from denying its own foundations. This kind of limitation is by no means peculiar to theology. Every discipline is bound to admit the reality of its own object and the conditions of accessibility of that object. No geologist, while remaining a geologist, can take the position that the earth does not exist or that it is unknowable. Astronomy cannot deny the heavens, optics cannot deny the light, and medicine cannot deny the fact of disease. As a human being, the theologian remains free to become an unbeliever, even an atheist, if so prompted by conscience. But in so doing, one automatically ceases to be a theologian. Let it not be said, therefore, that the theologian, as theologian, can reject revelation or that the Catholic theologian can reject the canonical Scriptures and dogmas of the church. The acceptance of these things is not a limitation on theology but rather the charter of its existence and freedom to be itself. The more firmly theology is grounded in faith, the more capable, generally speaking, will it be of understanding the nature and contents of faith.

Although Catholic theology must, as I have just said, submit to the word of God as it comes through Scripture, tradition, and the hierarchical magisterium, theology does not simply repeat what is in its sources. It reflects on the sources with a view to answering contemporary questions, questions not explicitly answered in the sources themselves. It seeks the intelligibility of the revelation in all the ways I have just indicated— through positive theology, that probes the sources; through apologetics, that seeks to establish credibility; through systematics, that concerns itself with the inner coherence of the whole scheme of revelation, and through practical theology, that ponders the implications of the revealed message for human conduct. Within its particular sphere of competence, theology is free to reach whatever conclusions are indicated by a proper application of its own method. Popes and bishops have no mandate to tell the theologian how to do theology, beyond the negative mandate of seeing to it that theology does not undermine the life of faith itself. Theology, therefore, possesses a certain freedom over against even the hierarchical magisterium. Without that freedom it could not be theology, and hence it could not be of service to the church. The medieval axiom, *non ancilla nisi libera*, holds for theology.

While emphasizing the fidelity of theology to the

teaching of the hierarchical magisterium, I have not ruled out the possibility of dissent. I recognize that in certain cases, which I would take to be rare in view of the overall reliability of the magisterium, a given theologian may find the official doctrine unconvincing. A proper docility will move the theologian to seek reasons in favor of the teaching in question, but there comes a point where the will cannot compel the intellect to assent, and where the possibility of an error in noninfallible magisterial teaching must be reckoned with. The approved theological manuals have for many years taken account of this eventuality, and since Vatican Council II, the United States bishops have put out guidelines for the public expression of dissenting positions in the church.[2]

Dissent should be neither glorified nor vilified. It is not necessarily an act of greater probity and courage to dissent than to assent. Whenever dissent is expressed it tends to weaken the church as a symbol of unity. Nevertheless, dissent cannot be totally eliminated. It may be subjectively and even objectively justified. To deny its existence or to seek to suppress it would be more harmful that to acknowledge it and deal with it honestly.

Theology always stands under correction. The hierarchical magisterium has the power and the responsibility to approve or disapprove of theological teaching from the standpoint of orthodoxy. By approving of the works of the fathers and doctors of the church, including saints such as Augustine and Thomas Aquinas, the church has given them a quasioffical status, so that the faithful may be confident that the works of these authors will lead them to a better grasp of the faith. But the magisterium never has canonized, and, I think, never could canonize, the theology of any school or individual. Just as faith differs from any systematization of faith, so the doctrine of the magisterium differs in its object from theology. Even when popes and bishops approvingly quote the works of theologians, they do not make the theology of these authors binding on the faithful.

The magisterium can associate certain theologians very closely with itself. Some, for example, are members of, or consultors to, the Congregation for the Doctrine of the Faith. Some are asked to draft papal encyclicals or other official documents. Some are given a canonical mission by their bishops to teach in seminaries or other ecclesiastical faculties. According to the Apostolic Constitution *Sapientia Christiana*, published by Pope John Paul II in 1979, those who teach with canonical mission "do not teach by their own authority but on the strength of a mission received from the Church" (art. 27 #1).

Occasionally one hears it said that professors have a canonical mission teach "in the name of the church." Although a proper interpretation can be given to this phrase, I prefer to avoid it, since it tends to obscure the distinction between the role of bishops, who by their teaching can publicly commit the church, and that of theologians, who cannot. Theology is, by its very nature, a private enterprise. A theologian who has a *nihil obstat* from the Holy See or a canonical mission or mandate from the competent authority is able to exercise his or her functions with the added prestige that comes from these tokens of official trust. But the theologian is not thereby dispensed from having to proceed according to the proper methods of the theological disciplines and from being subject to criticism from peers for any failures of scholarship or reasoning.

ACADEMIC FREEDOM

Up to this point I have been attempting to clarify what is meant by the teaching of the Catholic church. I have found it helpful to distinguish between the teaching *of* the church, which is that of the hierarchy, and teaching *in* the church, which is nonhierarchical. Both bishops and theologians teach, but they do so in different ways. Bishops teach with authority to bind in the name of

Christ; theologians teach in an academic, nonauthoritative way. I have spoken of the sense in which theology is bound to the doctrine of the official magisterium, and of the senses in which it is free. It will now be possible for me to turn, in the remainder of my paper, to the issue of academic freedom. Such freedom applies most obviously to teachers in the academy—that is to say, in institutions of higher learning—who are committed to exacting standards of scholarship. Is the theologian or the professor of other sacred disciplines, such as biblical studies and canon law, entitled to academic freedom, and if so, in what sense?

There is no official or uncontested definition of academic freedom. In current usage, at least in the United States, the term generally denotes the freedom of professionally qualified teachers, first, to pursue their scholarly investigations without interference; second, to publish the results of their research and reflection; and, third, to teach according to their own convictions, provided that they remain in the area of their competence and present the alternative positions with sufficient attention and fairness. Many statements on academic freedom add that in cases of dispute, the competence and professional conduct of the teacher should be assessed by experts chosen from among academic colleagues or peers.[3]

In the United States there is a strong tendency to maintain that academic freedom is essential to the very concept of a college or university. The American Association of University Professors (AAUP), in a series of statements since its inception in 1915, has promoted this position. Limitations on academic freedom are considered injurious to the academic standing of the institution, and likely to imperil the accreditation of its degrees by professional associations.[4] As the AAUP has recognized on several occasions, the concept of academic freedom raises delicate questions for church-related institutions. A Catholic college or university is not purely and simply an academy in the secular meaning of the term. It seeks to discharge a service toward the church and toward the religious development of its students, especially those who are themselves Catholics.[5]

One could object, of course, that any such practical orientation to goals that lie beyond the cultivation of rationally acquired knowledge is extraneous to the nature of the university. If so, theology, as I have explained it in this paper, would have no place in the university curriculum. This solution, as drastic as it is simple, is unrealistic. It rests upon a purist concept of the university that neglects the relation of education to the world as it is and to human beings as they are. The church and the Catholic people legitimately expect that some universities will provide an intellectual environment in which the meaning and implications of the faith can be studied in relation to the whole realm of human knowledge. Without Catholic university theology, the church would be less able to relate to the culture of the day and to reflect on its faith with the instruments of contemporary knowledge. Catholic parents and students often choose church-related colleges and universities because such institutions provide a favorable situation in which to gain a mature, reflective understanding of the faith.

If theology were expelled from the university, Catholic parents and students would be deprived of fundamental educational right. The church would be deprived of an important resource for its mission. The university, too, would suffer because, as Newman pointed out, other disciplines would occupy, without adequate warrant or competence, the territory vacated by the departure of theology.[6] The larger society would also stand to lose because in our pluralistic culture Catholic theological faculties provide valuable input from one of the major religious traditions of the nation.

It would be ironic indeed if university education, which arose in many parts of Europe under the sponsorship of the church, and which frequently looked upon theology as its crowning discipline, were now to

be defined in a way that excluded theology. It is an un-
deniable fact that many of the leading universities of the
world, both in the past and in our own day, have flour-
ished under ecclesiastical sponsorship and direction. It
would be sheer ignorance to deny the quality of scholarship that emanates from some of the major Catholic
universities and theological faculties in the United States
and in many other countries. To define university education so as to exclude such institutions and faculties
is evidence of a narrow parochialism that is, in its own
way, sectarian. If religious sectarianism is to be rejected—as indeed it should be—secular sectarianism should
not be established in its place.

Supposing, then, that theology as a systematic reflection upon faith *does* have a right to exist, at least in
some universities, we must inquire about the kind of
academic freedom that is desirable to protect this discipline. It does need protection. History provides abun-
dant cases in which civil and religious authorities have
unjustly intervened to prevent theologians from publish-
ing and teaching according to the canons of their own
discipline. Several years after the death of the Thomas
Aquinas, a number of his positions in philosophy and
theology were condemned by the bishop of Paris and the
archbishop of Canterbury. Some of his faithful followers were severely punished for heresy. Before long the
condemnations were withdrawn, but the very occur-
rence of the error illustrates the likelihood that local
episcopal authorities will be overzealous in seeking to
enforce orthodoxy. In modern times the authority of the
state has been even more oppressive than that of the
church in attempting to control theology. Consider, for
example, the actions of the *Parlement* of Paris and of
the Emperor Joseph II of Austria, not to mention the
excesses of German national socialism. Clearly, then,
theology stands to gain, as do other disciplines, from the
protection of academic freedom. But academic freedom
must be rightly understood.

The prevalent secular theories of academic freedom

are not fully satisfactory. They give rise to several difficulties. For example, these theories seem to imply that academic freedom absolves the Christian or Catholic theologian from the obligation to teach in accordance with the Christian or Catholic faith. Some theorists contend that no professor can be required to adhere to any substantive teaching. To set limits to scholarly conclusions, it is argued, is to violate a basic principle of academic freedom.[7]

This view of the matter, in my opinion, embodies some confusions. No one can be coerced into personally holding the faith. Faith is, by its very nature, free. But a rejection of Catholic faith, even if merely private, would be detrimental to theology as a reflection upon faith. A nonbelieving professor would be ill-suited to present the tradition of the church from the point of view of faith or to assist the student to reflect upon the implications of faith. In teaching according to his or her own convictions, such a professor could not be teaching Catholic theology. Thus a person hired for the purpose of teaching Catholic theology might well be disqualified by a failure to hold and profess the Catholic faith, especially if there were antipathy or resentment.

Further difficulties arise from the contention, frequently made, that alleged violations of the norms of Catholic theology should be judged only by colleagues, or "peers" as they are commonly called. It is not entirely clear who the peers of a Catholic theologian in a Catholic institution would be. Would they all be Catholics? Would they be theologians? If the question under dispute is whether a Catholic theologian has exceeded the bounds of orthodoxy, non-Catholics or non-theologians could hardly be qualified to reach a verdict. I would even doubt whether a group of Catholic theologians could be expected to render a truly objective judgment. Peer pressure would be too strong. According to a longstanding Catholic tradition, pastoral judgments concerning purity of doctrine are, in the last instance, the prerogative of the ecclesiastical magisterium.

I deliberately insert the words "in the last instance." For reasons already indicated, when I spoke of the condemnations of the Thomistic doctrine in France and England, I am apprehensive that bishops or their curial assistants, possibly aroused by one-sided letters of complaint, might pronounce overhastily upon technical questions in which they were not fully competent. They should make sure that they have correctly understood exactly what the theologian is saying and why. This will require a familiarity with the state of the discipline and the special meanings that certain terms have acquired in the literature of the field. Theologians need scope in which to develop tentative positions and to make hypothetical statements that could easily be misunderstood by nonspecialists. They are entitled to raise some legitimate questions about the current noninfallible teaching of the magisterium. They must, of course, be held to prudence in the ways in which they publicize their theories and hypotheses, but they cannot always be responsible for the uses that others make of statements quite proper in themselves.

To avoid perpetrating injustice, bishops may sometimes have the duty to enter into a dialogue process something like that suggested in the guidelines adopted by the U.S. bishops at their Seton Hall meeting in 1989. According to that document, "In cases of dispute, the theologian has the right to expect access to a fair process, protecting both substantive and procedural rights."[8] In a university, due process for its professors will normally be provided for by the statutes and the faculty manual.

Every theologian should enjoy academic freedom, in the sense of a right to inquire, publish and teach according to the norms of the discipline. But, because theology is an essentially ecclesial discipline, the freedom of the theologian must not be absolutized over and against other elements in the community of faith. While the freedom of the professor as an individual scholar should be respected, it should be seen in the context of other values. One such value is the integrity of Catholic theology as a meditation on the shared faith of the whole church. Whoever substitutes a purely individual or deviant faith forfeits any right to be called a Catholic theologian. Another such value is the maintenance of sound doctrine. Although sound doctrine is a particular responsibility of the hierarchical magisterium, it is of foundational importance for theology itself. In the interest of their own profession, theologians should support the magisterium as it seeks to safeguard the apostolic heritage, whether by way of positively encouraging sound developments or by way of administering, on occasion, a word of caution or correction. The rights of the theologian as an academician become real *only* when situated in this ecclesial framework.

I cannot on this occasion go into the complex question: how should the pastoral judgments of the hierarchy be implemented within the university? This question has to be answered in different ways for universities of different types. In each case the charter and statutes of the university must be considered, as well as the terms of the contract entered into between the university and the faculty member in question. Unless the statutes so provide, I do not see how the Holy See or the bishops could intervene directly in the working of a civilly chartered university by dismissing a professor or preventing a course from being taught. Whether the officers or trustees could dismiss a professor whom the hierarchy judged to be lacking in orthodoxy would depend upon the same variables just mentioned. On the other hand, a given university might by its statutes engage itself publicly to hire in its department of theology only professors who have received some kind of license or mission from ecclesiastical authorities. In the United States this type of arrangement will presumably be rare, and will normally be accompanied by provisions to assure due process. Here, as in other countries, ecclesiastical control can be, has been, and is fully compatible with a high level of theological research. Theologians of the stature of Rahner and Lonergan regularly taught, I believe, with a canonical mission or its equivalent.

I conclude, therefore, that the prevailing secular model, as described by standard authorities, requires some modification before being applied to Catholic or other church-related institutions. The model shows signs of having been constructed with the laudable but one-sided purpose of protecting university professors from incompetent outside authorities who might unjustly seek to impose their own ideas. This model overlooks the responsibility of theology to the community of faith and the mandate of the ecclesiastical magisterium to assure the doctrinal soundness of theology.

The secular model, moreover, is somewhat narrowly based on a theory of knowledge more suited to the empirical sciences than to theology, which rests primarily on divine revelation. The dogmas of faith do not have the same status in theology as the currently accepted theories have for secular science. Those who practice theology with the conviction that revealed truth exists and is reliably transmitted by authoritative sources will see the need to work out a properly *theological* concept of academic freedom. A properly adapted version will protect authentic theology but will not separate theologians from the body of the church; it will not set them in opposition to the community of faith or its pastoral leadership. Theologians and bishops, in spite of their different roles in the church, are fundamentally allies because they are alike committed to exploring the truth of God's revelation in Christ. The freedom of the teaching office and that of theology both have their roots in Christ, who is himself the truth that sets us free.

4. Academic Freedom and the University

Donald W. Wuerl

The role of a Catholic university and the place of academic freedom within a Catholic university are concepts not at all alien to Cardinal John Henry Newman. His masterful discourses to the Catholics of Dublin, as well as his occasional lectures and essays addressed to the members of the Catholic University so many years ago, ring true today in our discussion of Catholic intellectual life and academic freedom within the context of a Catholic university. I submit that Cardinal Newman's exposition is instructive for us today as we address the question of the Catholic model of academic freedom.

The Catholic concept of academic freedom is rooted in an ancient tradition that recognizes the faith seeking understanding. It is out of this tradition that Newman speaks and the outline of the Catholic university in his thought unfolds.

It is Newman's contention, so masterfully presented in his *Idea of a University*, that a true university—a place of growth in human wisdom on a universal, all-inclusive scale—must include theology as a branch of knowledge. "Religious doctrine," writes Newman, "is knowledge, in as full a sense as Newton's doctrine is knowledge. University teaching without theology is simply unphilosophical."[1] Yet the Catholic model of academic freedom faces strong and serious challenge now, as it did in his day, from other models of academic freedom that would empty the intellectual effort in a university setting of its theological content and direction.

I would like to explore the Catholic model of academic freedom in comparison with the present-day notion of academic freedom and offer an analysis of the elements of the Catholic model of academic freedom.

ACADEMIC FREEDOM

Traditionally academic freedom refers to the liberty of a person to carry on intellectual investigation in a scholarly manner within the structure of the academic community. In current secular terms, it is typically defined more narrowly as "the freedom of professionally qualified persons to inquire, discover, publish and teach the truth as they see it in the field of their competence, without any control of authority except the control of the authority of the rational methods by which truth is established."[2] It is the secular definition that serves as the model for much of the discussion today.

When considered in this way, as a process, it includes: 1) the unhindered freedom to explore a given subject to the extent that our rational powers of investigation are capable; and 2) the freedom to do so without influence or pressures external to the process.

This twofold definition, in turn, accepts several assumptions: 1) that human reason is the ultimate arbiter of all matters under investigation; 2) that the scientific method, that is, the study of empirical data, can alone yield truth; and 3) that no other voice, contribution or norm can be a determinant in the process.

Already this definition leads us to reflect on the ancient and useful distinction between theology and philosophy. Newman applies this general distinction to the Christian experience of revelation and the gift of the Holy Spirit. "Christianity differs," Newman points out in the *Essay on the Development of Christian Doctrine*, "from other religions and philosophies . . . not in kind, but in origin, not in nature, but in its personal characteristics, being informed and quickened by what is more than the intellect, by a Divine Spirit."[3]

What we say about scientific method for the philosopher cannot be said in the exact same univocal manner for the theologian. There are several viable working models of scholarly method. This is so for the obvious reason that theology uses as its starting point revelation which, of its nature, carries us beyond the limits of unaided reason. Hence, any definition of the freedom of investigation for the theologian includes, as internal to the process, revelation as both the starting point and the principle of verification.

The distinction between theology and philosophy underlines that there exists a variety of scholarly methods within the world of Christian academic effort and university experience. One methodology, for example, accepts the role of Scripture alone as normative. Another relies on Scripture as interpreted within a specific confessional tradition. The perennial Catholic scholarly method recognizes the role of Scripture, its scholarly interpretation and the function of the church in judging the validity of the interpretation.

The Catholic theological tradition includes as intrinsic to the process of theological development the voice of the teaching office (magisterium). The exercise of the office of bishop is not external or extraneous to the church's self-understanding but a vital and essential part of the process.[4]

REVELATION AND THE MAGISTERIUM

One of the major cornerstones of Roman Catholic "identity" is the communal character of faith. The church is not simply a collection of individuals who think and act the same way. The church, as the body of Christ, precedes the present gathering of individuals. The church's magisterium is a central part of the communal character of the faith and something that is of the very constitution of the church to provide it direction, stability, self-awareness and unity.

Christ's promise to remain with his church until the end of time takes on a special significance when we address the matter of the continual, authentic teaching of the truth of revelation. All in the church are called to spread the Word and receive gifts appropriate to their calling and baptismal character. It is necessary for the community as it grows and its members exercise their own gifts to maintain unity and the tie with the church of the apostles. As the gifts are given to build up the one church and as they derive from the one same Spirit, so they interrelate and must be coordinated. Individual gifts also need to be verified. The final judgment on the authenticity of any particular gift—or any particular teaching—rests with the bishops, who are charged to foster the unity of the church. There can be no unity with multiple, contradictory teachings.

Judgment does not mean that there is no discussion or even divergent views during the development of thought on a given subject, but at some point in dialogue, discussion and even disagreement give way to decision. We cross a line from discussion about various theological conclusions to the approbation and application of the conclusions. Here we find the real center of some of the present-day confusion and conflict—the distinction between the role and functions of bishops and theologians.

ACADEMIC FREEDOM IN ACTION

Today academic freedom has also come to include not only freedom of investigation and of expression, but also freedom to teach and to advocate a way of action. As presented today, the concept of academic freedom carries with it the idea of unlimited, unfettered freedom to express any thought, with its inherent consequences, and the concomitant right to propose theories as the basis for personal action.

It is this last point—the proposal of various teachings as the basis for alternate pastoral practice and an alternate Christian moral code—that raises particular difficulties for the church today and especially for Catholic universities.

In the model of academic freedom used historically in the church, freedom of discussion and investigation was one component of a much wider process that led to judgment about the authenticity of the teaching. In the ecclesial model of academic freedom the propositions of theologians do not automatically translate into authentic church teaching. Involved in the wider process is the recognition of the role of the Holy Spirit, which manifests itself in the *sensus fidei* of the faithful and the final approbation by the bishops. In this model the whole church participates in the process according to the gifts and ministries with which the Spirit blesses the church.

Newman stresses the continuity between and among the elements of the faith as the understanding of it develops. He quotes Vincent of Lerins in illustration of his point:

> Let the soul's religion ... imitate the law of the body, which as years go on, develops indeed and opens out its due proportions, and yet remains identically what it was. Small are a baby's limbs, a youth's are larger, yet they are the same.[5]

As the development of doctrine takes place in this model, the Spirit is recognized to move simultaneously on at least three levels: the study and penetration of faith and morals by theologians (whose authority derives not from their office, but from their skills of scholarship and the arguments they put forth to support their positions); the spiritual or almost intuitive grasp of the wholeness of the faith by the faithful; and the authoritative proclamation of the bishops, who have the pastoral care of the church as their ministry. The three realities are not the same and do not function in an identical way. All three are distinct yet complementary. Each can act as a reference point or corrective for the other in the process. Yet it remains for the office of bishop to pass final judgment (even if the judgment is not meant to be irreformable) on the authenticity of any specific teaching proposed as the faith and teaching of the church.

The ecclesial model provides for both development of the faith as well as a safeguard against the proliferation of teachings tailored to the secular influences of any one area or culture, no matter how much popularity the new teaching might enjoy.

THEOLOGICAL DEVELOPMENT

Obviously there is no need for judgment about a theological development unless such development occurs. The Catholic theological tradition carries on the task of penetrating the mystery of faith and of deepening our grasp of the revealed Word of God. Hence, the honored and important role that theologians play in the life of the church. Theology attempts to respond to changing human realities in a way that reflects new insights into the human condition and the development of the human sciences while integrating them with the church's tradition of wisdom and the absolute claims of revelation. Theologians exercise a ministry of service for the good of the whole church.

It is here that we also locate the necessary distinction

between personal opinion and the authoritative proclamation of the church. Perhaps we should also underline
that we are not talking about personal conscience and
how one acts in good conscience, but church teaching
and how one forms a correct conscience.

Personal opinion, by itself, is not a sufficient basis for
the formation of a correct Catholic conscience. Catholic
teaching is. At this juncture we encounter the critical
question: Who in the Catholic church—after all the
dialogue, discernment and, perhaps, even disagreement—
who in the long process of theological investigation,
conflicting views and synthesis—who makes the final
judgment about the teaching and pastoral practice of the
church? The bishops (after appropriate consultation,
dialogue and discernment) or individual believers?

VALUES SERVED BY ACADEMIC FREEDOM

As we examine the meaning of academic freedom, three
questions come to mind:

1. What is its purpose and goal?
2. Are there limits, either internal or external, to the
process within which this freedom is exercised?
3. How is this freedom related to other realities in the
church?

The purpose of freedom of investigation is to permit
scholarship. The ultimate goal of the process is truth.
Academic freedom is not a goal in itself, but a necessary part of the climate in which scientific investigation
and intellectual development can prosper. In every
scientific process there must be the freedom to explore
and develop theories as well as to rest those teachings
which are accepted and in place.

STRUCTURE OF ACADEMIC FREEDOM

Scientific investigation is also circumscribed by limits
internal to every study. The laws of physics (e.g., gravity),

the laws of chemistry (e.g., elemental weights), or mathematical rules (e.g., identity of numbers), all set limits to scientific theory. This is part of the very nature of the science, as are revelation and the teaching of the church for theology. The recognition of such limits does not halt the scientific advance. Rather, it permits fruitful and real development. What is harmful is limitation imposed from outside for reasons other than the quest for truth.

In an analogous manner we can speak of the similarity with the function of the Supreme Court in the world of American jurisprudence and law, particularly constitutional law. The intervention of the Supreme Court and its decisions are not an intrusion by an outside, extraneous force but the articulation of an intrinsic aspect of American development of law. Within the Catholic development of theology, the magisterium exercises a like intrinsic function.

There is a profoundly human value served by the respectful attention that should be paid to the power of reason. We are endowed, uniquely of all the species, with the capacity to understand and reason. We can deal with abstract concepts and formulate propositions that open us onto the truth. Hence, reason must be respected and its conclusions accepted. To act otherwise is to act arbitrarily. To ignore the dictates of reason is to act in a less than fully human manner.

At the same time, we must not take the simplistic position that every conclusion proposed by science and technology is in itself absolutely truthful and self-evidently right. Science is limited to working on the data available. The quality of any human judgment can be no better than the completeness of the data. Nor is application and appreciation of data free from the influences of passion and prejudice. While extolling the virtues of science, we should not allow our adulation to blind us to the sad facts of the human condition. Reason is a faculty, not a deity.

JUDGMENT CONCERNING THE TRUTH

In every rational process we reach the point where a judgment is made. The judgment may be one concerning the truth or falsity of a proposition or the rightness or wrongness of some action. This is a key concept because all investigation eventually comes to a moment of judgment making.

Secular science is concerned with the validity or integrity of the intellectual process in the conviction that there is no other recourse to arrive at truth.

Catholic theology is convinced that truth (not the fullest possible expression of all truth—but truth) has its ultimate foundation in God and is communicated to us also in revelation.

Both science and theology seek the truth. Both accept the validity of intellectual investigation. Yet theology assumes a point of verification for its judgments. Secular science, by its nature, does not have this point of reference and, hence, must accept multiple judgments as true as long as the validity of the intellectual process can be sustained. Even in theological traditions that accept revelation but not the teaching office of the church there is a tendency, verified historically, to diversity rather than oneness in the faith.

Both science and Catholic theology respect the process of intellectual investigation in a climate of academic freedom. Theology, however, includes as internal to its process both the demands of revelation and the exercise of the bishops' teaching office. As our holy father points out:

> The bishops of the church, as *doctores et magistri fidei* (doctors and teachers of the faith), should not be seen as external agents but as participants in the life of the Catholic university in its privileged role as protagonist in the encounter between faith and science and between revealed truth and culture.[6]

Cardinal Newman expresses the same idea in this manner:

> It is no sufficient security for the Catholicity of a university, even that the whole of Catholic theology should be professed in it, unless the church breathes her own pure and unearthly spirit into it, and fashions and molds its organization, and watches over its teaching and knits together its pupils and superintends its action.[7]

SCHOLARSHIP AND THE CATHOLIC UNIVERSITY

Does adherence to the magisterium mean that creative scholarship is impossible? History would seem to indicate that the theological endeavor has prospered well within the church under the tutelage of the teaching office.

Does the role of revelation and teaching office of the bishops preclude the very idea of a Catholic university? Historically this has not been the case and is only recently raised in our country, but more in terms of funding than faith value and identity issues.

Then why the tension between some elements in the church today and the teaching office over the question of what constitutes Catholic teaching and the freedom necessary to express and develop the teaching?

It seems to me that much of the tension comes from what might be called a limited focus—to focus on only one aspect of the discussion or on only one model of academic freedom. There is a need to keep all the elements of the discussion in proper focus to have a correct view of the whole picture.

To focus exclusively on the repetition of the faith as found in Scripture and in previously formulated statements of the teaching office may be a good catechetical device, but it would not encourage necessary and healthy theological development. New situations, qualitative changes in society and problems raised by contemporary technology require our attention and study. The work of the theologian allows the church to grow and face the ever-new circumstances of the faith.

To focus solely on freedom of personal expression loses sight of the fact that the starting point of theological investigation and its major point of referral includes the teaching office. The exercise of this office is essential to good theological growth because it is internal to the science of theology.

To focus on theologians and bishops as antagonists loses sight of their different yet complementary tasks. Their interaction should enrich and enlighten both theologians and bishops.

To focus on the secular model of academic freedom and to view its agnostic presuppositions as a substitute for the Catholic tradition of "faith seeking understanding" loses sight of centuries of fruitful intellectual development in the Western world.

To focus on the bishops' teaching office solely as a corrective function loses the wider vision of the prophetic role of the teaching church and also of the healing, saving effect of that proclamation.

To focus on the university status of the theologian as if this places the theologian outside or above the church loses sight of the reality that all the faithful—including bishops, teachers, theologians, scholars and candidates for the priesthood—owe, as we are reminded by the Second Vatican Council, "religious assent of soul" to the bishops when they speak in the name of Christ.[8]

ROLE OF THE THEOLOGIAN

This does not mean that efforts at theological advances must await the intervention of the teaching office at each stage of development. Theology has both an obligation and right to continue its studies and investigations. In fact, it is usually within the world of theological discussion—sometimes heated—that a great deal of the insight later recognized as fruitful development has taken and continues to take place. A necessary component of this discussion is the self-critique within the theological community. The ability and willingness of various theologians and schools of theology to critique each other's works and theories are vital to the development of theology. Without critique, there is no theological pluralism. Unfortunately, in the past years useful and reforming critique in much of the world of theology has been left to the teaching office. This represents a shift in focus for both theology and the teaching office.

COOPERATION AMONG BISHOPS AND THEOLOGIANS

Freedom of inquiry into the meaning of the faith is all the more enhanced through the cooperation of bishops and theologians as both recognize the role of the Spirit in actively guiding the growth of the church, inspiring development in the understanding of God's Word, while at the same time preserving the church from error through the exercise of the teaching office.

The work of theological development is to push our understanding of the faith to new and more profound limits. It is the task of the bishops to note when the limits have been crossed.

The two extremes that the teaching office and the theologians together seek to avoid are either the stagnation of our understanding of God's Word or the substitution of any one personal opinion for Christ's teaching. For those in priestly formation work, the goal is to prepare future priests to respond in the name and with the voice of the church to the practical, pastoral needs of the faithful.

CHURCH'S TRADITIONAL ROLE

The church's commitment to the truth has no better witness than the world of universities which, in Western civilization, owe their birth, life and sustenance to the Catholic Church.

As Pope John Paul II reaffirmed:

> To appreciate fully the value of (our) heritage, we need to recall the origins of Catholic university life. The university as we know it began in close association with the church. This was no accident. Faith and love of learning have a close relationship. . . . Religious faith itself calls for intellectual inquiry; and the confidence that there can be no contradiction between faith and reason is a distinctive feature of the Catholic humanistic tradition as it existed in the past and as it exists in our own day.[9]

The underlying reason for the church's respect for the power of the intellect is the church's firm belief that it is the truth that makes us free. Freedom from error, freedom from ignorance, freedom from doubt are both the motive and the fruit of the church's ancient and traditional commitment to the life of the intellect.

We have always accepted the truth of Jesus' proclamation that he is the truth come from his Father. Within a century of Christ's death and resurrection, efforts were already at work to develop, explore and adapt the Gospel message to various cultures and systems of philosophy and thought. This has gone on in each age down to our day. There is a very real sense in which it is true to say that the church and intellectual development are mother and daughter.

In short, is there an inherent conflict between the exercise of freedom in scholarship committed to the pursuit of truth and such activity within a Catholic university? I believe the answer to be very clearly and demonstrably "no!"

We fully believe that the father of Jesus is the God of creation . . . who gives us our intellect and the freedom to use it . . . while also revealing to his church that God is the truth and Christ both the way and the truth . . . which, like God, is One.

5 • The Nature of Academic Freedom and the Teaching of Theology

William J. Byron, S.J.

There are perhaps as many descriptions of academic freedom as there are academics at work in the academy. My task here is twofold—first, to get at the *nature* of academic freedom and thus closer to a genuine definition than a mere description; second, to apply the idea of academic freedom to the teaching of theology. This second task raises the question of an ecclesial limit on academic freedom.

The nature of academic freedom applies to those conditions or circumstances wherein a structured teaching-learning transaction can take place. Academic freedom resides in persons—teachers and learners—who meet in a setting designed to foster disciplined inquiry. What happens there is the exploration and communication of knowledge.

Sometimes no one is there but the investigator, the lone researcher seeking further understanding of an identifiable dimension of truth. Academic freedom protects the isolated investigator. Sometimes many people are present, often as students receiving instruction, frequently as coinvestigators searching for new understandings. Academic freedom protects all participants in any given teaching-learning transaction.

What is academic freedom? Freedom in the academy is an environment. It is a defined environment bounded by academic competence, human prudence, personal integrity, professional standards and peer judgment. It is, therefore, not an unlimited freedom. Academic freedom is an environment within which personal and institutional autonomy remain open to outside influence but protected from outside control. Finally, academic freedom is an environment dependent upon and expressive of an academic institution's charter and mission statement.

Why have academic freedom? To protect the disciplined inquirer from the unwelcome whims or reprisals of powerful others who may disagree with his or her views. That is quite different, of course, from the welcome outcome of having one's views displaced by better evidence or sounder reasoning. Academic freedom provides a needed measure of employment security to professionals whose ideas might displease their academic employers. It also is intended to assure students access to all legitimate fonts of knowledge. Intellectual discovery and growth in understanding prosper in noncoercive environments. Academic freedom guarantees such an environment to teachers and learners.

In any academic context, however, there are *limits* on academic freedom. First, there is the limit of truth itself. Teachers are not free to profess falsehood. Next, a limit is imposed by the canons and associated competencies that the community of scholars expects to find in a given academic discipline. Disciplined inquiry implies, first of all, responsible inquiry, and then competent communication of the results of inquiry. Another limit on academic freedom is human prudence, especially with respect to the communication of truths that would not be appropriately communicated in certain circumstances or to members of certain age groups. These limits apply and are acknowledged to belong wherever the academy functions.

The question facing Catholic colleges and universities today concerns the freedom of inquiry and communication of theological knowledge on a Catholic campus in light of the institution's relationship, however indirect, to a hierarchical church. Is there an ecclesial limit on academic freedom? Can there be an acceptable constraint on investigation, but, more importantly, on the communication of truth on a Catholic campus because of the church relationship? Moreover, what happens to academic freedom when a question of truth or error is decided *outside* the academy?

I believe there can be and is an ecclesial limit on academic freedom. Further, this ecclesial limit need not violate academic freedom so long as a church-related institution, whether Catholic or not, understands itself to be also faith-related, and faith, on that campus, is shared by many and respected by all. Faith, of course, is a gift of God freely accepted by the believing person. Acceptance of limits associated with religious faith suggests to me not a denial of freedom but the exercise of freedom, the freedom of religious commitment.

If faith is first, last and always a gift—and Catholic theology is unambiguous in so describing it—language regarding the communication of an understanding of faith must be used with care lest "teaching the faith" be thought of in images of transfusion or injection. Faith, the ineffable gift that draws one into contact with a God of mystery, can nonetheless, and up to a point, be explained. At least the tenets of a faith community—those formulations of religious truth that are held by members of a faith community—can be articulated in their present stage of development, located in their scriptural foundations, and analyzed at different stages of historical controversy, philosophical expression and official ecclesiastical formulation.

Reflection on past understandings is only part of the work of a theologian. Development of new and deeper understandings is a special responsibility. This is the professional and scientific expression of *fides quaerens intellectum* for theologians in the church. The ecclesial limit on this exercise of human understanding in the church is continuity with the tradition of the church. The tradition, however, is a living and growing reality. Hence the ecclesial limit on a theologian's academic freedom is more viaduct than retaining wall. It is, in any case by whatever metaphor, a limiting factor.

Discontinuity would mean, by definition, a break of greater or lesser propositions from the tradition, a separation from the faith community. Hence the development of new, better and deeper understandings can always expect to confront an ecclesial limit, a protective layer or buffer zone intended to prevent breaks. This need not be an insurmountable barrier to inquiry nor a clamp on communication. Instead it can serve to remind the communicator that the *teaching of Catholic theology is not communication only, but communion with the community of faith* that his or her theology is intended to serve. That faith community, in the case of Roman Catholicism, is organized hierarchically with clear lines of authority. It is consistent with Catholic principles to have ecclesiastical authority exercised in a way that *authors*—in the sense of encouraging, enabling and drawing out—the creative potential of theologians in the church, encouraging the exploration of ideas and fostering the development of what will eventually become official Catholic doctrine. Such "authorship" on the part of the church authorities would always look to continuity with the tradition. *Continuity* will function as the ecclesial limit on the academic freedom of theologians in the church.

Who is to decide whether a given development represents a continuous advance of tradition or a discontinuous break? Who is to determine whether a Catholic theologian is in or out of communion with the teaching church in his or her efforts to advance the tradition? And how can these judgments find their proper place within the Catholic college or university, thus protecting the institution's autonomy and the professor's integrity as a free academic working within appropriate limits? The answer to this last question presupposes an answer to the question of Catholic identity: what, in fact, makes a university or college Catholic?

In my view, theologians and bishops should together examine questions of continuity or break; then the bishops should decide. I also think theologians and bishop should together examine whether or not a theologian is in or out of communion with the teaching church when the theologian offers theories or theses intended to advance the tradition. The formal determination remains the province of the bishop. If the final determination is, in fact, the province of the bishop, how can the institution where that theologian works be said to be autonomous? It is autonomous by virtue of the identity it has chosen for itself. It has a freely chosen Catholic character expressed in its mission statement and subscribed to by the campus community. The internalization of this Catholic identity includes institutional acceptance of all things Catholic as congenial to the range of inquiry on campus, and nothing Catholic is viewed as foreign to the enterprise. The range of interest goes far beyond the Catholic, of course, but the point to note is that nothing Catholic can be excluded. The assertion of institutional autonomy in the face of an ecclesial limit on academic freedom is, therefore, no denial of academic freedom. It simply points to an identity—internal, freely chosen, and accepted by all in the campus community (as distinguished from the broader faith community)—which acknowledges a role for church authority in doctrinal matters. Those who choose not to accept, or no longer subscribe to the Catholic identity of the institution, do not necessarily disqualify themselves from the faith community, but they do not separate themselves from identification with the campus community. To identify with an institution without accepting that institution's self-proclaimed identity makes no sense. To proclaim a Catholic identity without accepting an ecclesial limit on theological exploration and communication is to misunderstand not only the nature of church-relatedness, but also the idea of a university and the meaning of academic freedom.

In his preface to *The Idea of a University*, John Henry Newman noted that when the church founds a university, she is not cherishing talent, genius, or knowledge, for their own sake, but for the sake of her children, with a view to their spiritual welfare and their religious influence and usefulness, with the object of training them to fill their respective posts in life better, and of making them more intelligent, capable active members of society."[1] In the first of his nine "Discourses" on "University Teaching" (for all practical purposes, chapter 1 in part 1 on *The Idea of a University*), Newman comments on the role of ecclesiastical authority in the establishment of a Catholic university.

> "Ecclesiastical authority, not argument, is the supreme rule and the appropriate guide for Catholics in matters of religion. It has always the right to interpose, and sometimes, in the conflict of parties and opinions, it is called on to exercise that right. It has lately exercised it in our own instance: it has interposed in favor of a pure University system for Catholic youth, forbidding compromise or accommodation of any kind. Of course its decision must be heartily accepted and obeyed, and that the more, because the decision proceeds, not simply

from the Bishops of Ireland, great as their authority is, but from the highest authority on earth, from the Chair of St. Peter."

To that, Newman adds: "Moreover, such a decision not only demands our submission, but has a claim upon our trust."[2] And the basis for this trust?

"It is the decision of the Holy See; St. Peter has spoken, it is he who has enjoined that which seems to us so un-promising. He has spoken, and has a claim on us to trust him. He is no recluse, no solitary student, no dreamer about the past, no doter upon the dead and gone, no projector of the visionary. He for eighteen hundred years has lived in the world; he has seen all fortunes, he has encountered all adversaries, he has shaped himself for all emergencies. If ever there was a power on earth who had an eye for the times, who has confined himself to the practicable, and has been happy in his anticipations, whose words have been facts, and whose commands prophecies, such is he in the history of ages, who sits from generation to generation in the Chair of the Apostles, as the Vicar of Christ, and the Doctor of His Church."[3]

These views may seem quaint, even naive, to the pres-ent-day reader who turns to Newman with a wide open mind and the best of will. But they help to explain why Newman had no hesitation in stating that "ecclesiasti-cal authority, not argument, is the supreme rule and the appropriate guide for Catholics in matters of religion." Nor does Newman claim here that the pope is always right, just that the Catholic will never go wrong by trust-ing him.

It would be safe to presume that Newman's evident respect and trust of the church's influence relative to the founding of a university would extend to a special role for the church in the theological life of the university. Much later in his book, in a chapter on "Duties of the Church Towards Knowledge," he writes:

"[T]he Church has no call to watch over and protect Science; but towards Theology she has a distinct duty:

it is one of the special trusts committed to her keeping. Where Theology is, there she must be; and if a University cannot fulfill its name and office without the recognition of Revealed Truth [a point argued earlier in the book], she must be there to see that it is a *bona fide* recognition, sincerely made and consistently acted on."[4]

Those who dismiss the notion of a Catholic university as a contradiction in terms will be relieved perhaps to note that the great theoretician of Catholic higher education assigns a "watch over" function—quite literally, an *episcopus* or "episcopal" role—to the church *only* in the area of theology. They might wonder how that episcopal role can be implemented without impinging on the autonomy of the university, and that question raises again the issue of identity. Being open to all things Catholic (one way of expressing Catholic identity) means being open to episcopal oversight in the area of theology.

Without appearing to be excessively defensive, and certainly without adopting an offensive attack as the best defensive measure, the "contradiction-in-terms" Catholic university might fairly ask its secular counterparts how they can claim university status—*Studium Generale* or "School of Universal Learning" would be Newman's designation—if their disciplined inquiry makes no systematic pursuit of revealed truth. Some would reply that they are simply not interested in theology. Others would point to ongoing teaching and research in religious studies taking place on their campuses. For a variety of reasons—legal on the part of state universities, preference in the independent sector—many universities will not conduct disciplined inquiry and communication of religious truth with fidelity to any particular faith tradition. There, of course is the opening the church-related college or university wants to fill.

Since no one thinks it strange to have state universities with identities drawn from geographic boundaries, with special service relationship to the citizens of their respective states, with openness to state influence, dependence on state funding, and daily challenges to their autonomy from outside pressures that threaten to translate influence into control, why should it be regarded as unusual to have private universities with church-related identities and relationship to a faith community that parallel the public institutions' relationships to the civic community? It is, of course, not unusual, as the widespread presence of church-related higher education in the United States—with its constitutional guarantee of the free exercise of religious commitment—attests. Both state-related and church-related universities will always need the protection of academic freedom against undue external influences. Both types of institution will first, by virtue of their respective charters, have internalized control vested in a governing board. And both types can welcome or withstand *external* influence by exercising, as they wish, their chartered autonomy. Autonomy simply means that the governing board makes its own decisions, under its charter, in pursuit of its educational mission. And finally, all types of institutions of higher learning, not just those interested in theology, would be expected to provide the protection of academic freedom against undue *internal* influence, including undue influence from the governing board.

Why should those who think theology is integral to university life appear to be on the defensive in our day? Probably because of the dogmatism of science in contemporary higher education. "Scientists believe in science in the same way that the majority of Catholics believe in the Church, namely as Truth crystallized in an infallible collective opinion," wrote *Simone Weil*; "they contrive to believe this in spite of the continual changes in theory. In both cases it is through lack of faith in God." This biting comment is recorded by Robert Coles in *Simone Weil: A Modern Pilgrimage*.[5] "A Catholic directs his thought secondarily towards the truth, but primarily toward conformity with the church's doctrine," argued Weil; she then added: "A scientist does the same, only in this case there is no established doctrine but a collective opinion in the process of formation." And

Coles comments: "That collective opinion can be not only helpful and instructive to those anxious to learn more, but also an instrument of control, a means by which compliance is exacted and disagreement punished." Sad to say, science has become the most emphatic expression of the extraordinarily secular tone of contemporary society.

I am not lamenting the existence of authorities—persons of superior intellect—in the scientific community. I wish we had more of them. Nor am I suggesting that there should be no authorities by virtue of intellect alone in the theological community. I wish we had more of them. I am lamenting the attitude, the kind of peer pressure that has emerged from the environment of physical and life sciences, that displays a bias against, or ar least an indifference toward, the spiritual, the immaterial, the religious and theological realities of life.

Neither physical science nor theology can pressure to be free of pressures, influences, limits and controls within the academy. Both science and theology belong in the academy. Each depends on the other if it is to realize its full potential. Neither should underestimate the other's concern for objectivity and freedom from inappropriate control. And in considering the critique of Simone Weil, Catholics should note their companionship with scientists in her sweeping charge that *both* suffer from a lack of faith in God. Those who feel the impulse for control of Catholic theology should "walk humbly" as they attempt to see, in specific matters theological, just how God's authority is to be ascertained.

Secular academics might fairly invite religions educators, in the interest of preservation of the idea of a university, to keep a watchful eye on the line between influence and control, as all universities must. And the church-related institutions, grateful for the opportunity to exist freely here in America, are quite willing to write control along with religious identity into their civil charters. Under their charters, control is exercised by a duly constituted board of trustees, which in all cases must respect both due process and academic freedom. Outside the charter, and from a variety of off-campus command posts, the impulse for control will probably always find the college or university campus a desirable target. That says a great deal about the importance of the idea that has evolved over the centuries into what we call a university. It is so important an idea that the church, the state and various other entities sacrifice to make it their own and vie with one another to make their embodiment of the idea the best.

In Catholic circles, the impulse for control by ecclesiastical authorities focuses on theology, the central element of the institution's Catholic identity. Here again, Newman can be helpful. In fact, his entire chapter on "Christianity and Scientific Investigation" could well serve as a preamble to discussion between bishops and theologians once they find the right structure for joint participation in theological dialogue. "[T]here must be great care taken to avoid scandal," writes Newman, "or shocking the popular mind, or unsettling the weak; the association between truth and error being so strong in particular minds that it is impossible to weed them of the error without rooting up the wheat with it."[6]

Newman continues:

> I am not, then supposing the scientific investigator (1) to be *coming into collision with dogma;* nor (2) venturing, by means of his investigations, upon any interpretation of Scripture, or upon other conclusion in *the matter of religion;* nor (3) of his *teaching,* even in his own science, paradoxes, when he should be investigating and proposing; nor (4) of his recklessly *scandalizing the weak;* but, these explanations being made I still say that a scientific speculator or inquirer is not bound, in conducting his researches, to be every moment adjusting his course by the maxims of the schools or by popular traditions, or by those of any other science distinct from his own, or to be ever narrowly watching what those external science have to say to him, or to be determined to be edifying, or to be ever answering heretics and unbelievers; being

confident, from the impulse of generous faith, that, however his line of investigation may swerve now and then, and vary to and fro in its course, or threaten momentary collision or embarrassment with any other department of knowledge, theological or not, yet, if he lets it alone, it will be sure to come home, because truth never can really be contrary to truth, and because often what at first sight is an "exception," in the event most emphatically *"probat regulam."*[7]

Newman quite literally underlines the importance of what I referred to earlier as prudence and respect for the canons of scientific discipline when I identified limits on academic freedom. Truth also is a limit, as I noted above. What, then, can be said about error in this regard?

"[I]n scientific researches error may be said, without a paradox, to be in some instances the way to truth, and the only way. Moreover, it is not often the fortune of any one man to live through an investigation; the process is one of not only many stages, but of many minds. What one begins, another finishes; and a true conclusion is at length worked out by the cooperation of independent schools and the perseverance of successive generations. This being the case, we are obliged, under the circumstances, to bear for awhile with what we feel to be error, in consideration of the truth in which it is eventually to issue."[8]

In perhaps his strongest expression of feeling on this point, Newman exclaims, "Let us eschew secular history, and science, and philosophy for good and all, if we are not allowed to be sure that Revelation is so true that the altercations and perplexities of human opinion cannot really or eventually injure its authority."[9] The question then, of course, becomes: what, in fact, is included in divine revelation? What form must a theological declaration take to indicate that a given doctrine is proposed for belief as belonging to the body of divine revelation?

"Great minds need elbowroom," writes Newman, "not indeed in the domain of faith, but of thought. And so indeed do lesser minds, and all minds."[10] The theologian, like a scientific investigator, operates within constraints. His or her "elbowroom" will have an ecclesial limit, namely, continuity with the tradition, especially at what John Courtney Murray used to call its "growing edge." Newman has a final word directed specifically to theologians:

> [W]hat I would venture to recommend to theologians . . . is a great and firm belief in the sovereignty of Truth. Error may flourish for a time, but Truth will prevail in the end. The only effect of error ultimately is to promote Truth. . . . On the other hand, it must be of course remembered, Gentlemen, that I am supposing all along good faith, honest intentions, a loyal Catholic spirit, and a deep sense of responsibility. I am supposing, in the scientific inquirer, a due fear of giving scandal, of seeming to countenance views which he does not really countenance, and of siding with parties with whom he heartily differs. I am supposing that he is fully alive to the existence and the power of the infidelity of the age; that he keeps in mind the moral weakness and the intellectual confusion of the majority of men; and that he has no wish at all that any one soul should get harm from certain speculations today, though he may have the satisfaction of being sure that those speculations will, as far as they are erroneous or misunderstood, be corrected in the course of the next half-century.[11]

With those words, Newman ends his essay on "Christianity and Scientific Investigation." Those same words, it seems to me, would be a useful keynote to open regional and even local exchanges between bishops and theologians as they attempt to come to a common understanding of the ecclesial limits on the disciplined theological inquiry that the bishops and the rest of the church urgently need, and that Catholic theologians, from their positions within the academy, are ready to provide.

Pope John Paul II addressed an assembly of U.S. Catholic college and university administrators in New Orleans at Xavier University on 12 September 1987. He spoke to the issue of what makes a Catholic college or university Catholic. In his view, Catholic identity "depends upon the explicit profession of Catholicity on the part of the university as an institution, and also upon the personal conviction and sense of mission on the part of its professors and administrators." The pope looks to these institutions to help "to make the Church's presence felt in the world of culture and science." Meeting this challenge requires "the personal conviction and sense of mission" of professors and administrators, those mainly responsible for the articulation and implementation of the Catholic identity. And later in his New Orleans address, with the simple assertion that "religious faith itself calls for intellectual inquiry," the pope assumes that there should be theological inquiry—faith seeking understanding—on a Catholic campus. "[T]hat there can be no contradiction between faith and reason is a distinctive feature of the Catholic humanistic tradition." Since the Catholic university "is dedicated to the service of truth...,

> there is an intimate relationship between the Catholic university and the teaching office of the Church. The bishops of the Church, as *Doctores et Magistri Fidei*, should be seen not as external agents but as participants in the life of the Catholic university in its privileged role as protagonist in the encounter between faith and science and between revealed truth and culture.

Bishops and theologians alike must enable the Gospel always to "challenge the accomplishment and assumptions of the age,"[12] so that the Gospel can "purify the culture, uplift it, and orient it to the service of what is authentically human. Humanity's very survival may depend on it." Required of both bishop and theologian is "fidelity to the word of God, to ensure that human progress takes into account the entire revealed truth of the external act of love in which the universe and especially the human person acquire ultimate meaning." But how is this relationship between bishop and theologian to work out in practice? The pope sees it this way:

> Theology is at the service of the whole ecclesial community. The work of theology involves an interaction among the various members of the community of faith. The bishops, united with the Pope, have the mission of authentically teaching the message of Christ; as pastors they are called to sustain the unity in faith and Christian living of the entire People of God. In this they need the assistance of Catholic theologians, who perform an inestimable service to the Church. But theologians also need the charism entrusted by Christ to the bishops and, in the first place, to the Bishop of Rome. The proof of their work, in order to enrich the life-stream of the ecclesial community, must ultimately be tested and validated by the Magisteruim. In effect, therefore, the ecclesial context of Catholic theology gives it a special character and value even when theology exists in an academic setting.

A structure is needed in every Catholic college to facilitate participation by the local bishops in the theological dialogue of the college, not in the governance of the college but in the theological discussion and debate that are part of the life of the college or university. This should be a reciprocal influence of theologian on bishop and bishop on theologian, as faith continues its quest for understanding. An appropriate teaching-learning structure, respectful of this desired reciprocity, is needed. Perhaps the seminar room, as opposed to the lecture hall, is an appropriate model that will foster the kind of exchange that is desirable. A roundtable, "horizontal" model is natural to a campus. It is properly collegial and certainly preferable to a one-way, "vertical" delivery system of judgments and conclusions from bishop to theologians, or vice versa. Any on-campus collegial model is superior to the distant and detached exchange characteristic of correspondence schools. The post office is no substitute for direct dialogue. Theologians and bishops have to get together for the exploration of all theological questions. If they do, they will surely grow in love and respect for one another, and in their understanding of the revelation God has entrusted to his Church. In this way bishops can, as the holy father suggests, be "participants in the life of the Catholic university in its privileged role as protagonist in the encounter between faith and science and between revealed truth and culture."

Such participation would do no violence to institutional autonomy. Outsiders from the fields of law, medicine, business, the arts and countless other fields of knowledge are routinely invited to participate in intellectual exchanges on campus. Nor, in my view, would the fact that the outcome of this fully participatory theological reflection "must ultimately be tested and validated by the magisteruim" necessarily imply an infringement on academic freedom. Outside courts validate legal theories debated on campuses. Outside agencies license drugs tested in university laboratories. Patents and copyrights are granted to professors by outside authorities. That Catholic theology should be "tested and validated" by off-campus ecclesiastical authorities is, of course, a special case involving only Catholic theologians and Catholic campuses, but not so special as to disqualify the Catholic campus from membership in the larger set of special cases that make up the world of American higher education.

A question that cannot be avoided on the side of ecclesiastical authorities relates to the preparedness and willingness of bishops to participate in dialogue with academic theologians. Not all bishops are theologians. Nor have all bishops who hold academic degrees in theology "kept up" with developments sufficiently to qualify them for participation in academic dialogue. Another way of posing the problem raised by the pope's New Orleans proposal is to suggest that bishops will now have to be attentive to their personal bibliographies. In order to participate in theological dialogue, one must be a contributor to theological reflection. One's own reflection, one's understanding of the tradition, one's

insight relative of clarifying or advancing the tradition—
all these must be articulated and communicated to the
other participants in the dialogue. The traditional way
of communicating these insights is through the delivery
of papers and the publication of manuscripts. Bishops
who are not academics would not, of course, be expected
to have bibliographies that would rival those of the
professors. (Some bishops might quip that they are where
they are because of the way they chose, at an earlier
career stage, to handle the publish or parish option!) But
bishop participants in theological dialogue should be
willing to put their thoughts on paper. That paper would
be shared, before the dialogue begins, with the theologian
participants, just as the writings of the theologians would
be in the hands of the bishops by the way of preparation
for the structured dialogue. If a bishop is incapable of
articulating and presenting his theological reflection in
this way, it seems to me that he therefore disqualifies
himself from participation in the theological life of the
Catholic university and, more importantly, he recuses
himself from judging the quality of the theological reflection of others. He can, of course, make his own the
judgments about quality and even orthodoxy rendered
by others; bishops are, after all, to be judges of orthodoxy,
not of theology as such. But then what would be the
intellectual grounds he could claim for inclusion in that
key sentence in the holy father's speech in New Orleans?
"The bishops of the church, as *Doctores et Magistri Fidei*,
should be seen not as external agents but as participants
in the life of the Catholic university in its privileged role
as protagonist in the encounter between faith and science
and between revealed truth and culture."

Typically and quite properly, the concern of the bishop
will be centered on the pastoral implications of what
emerges from theological reflection. There is no better
place to register that concern than in the process of
theological reflection within the university.

To invite the participation of a bishop in theological
discussion on campus is not to presume that differences

between a local bishop and a given theologian over what constitutes sound Catholic doctrine would immediately become grounds for action against the theologian. The whole point of putting a structure for discussion in place is to create common ground for fuller understanding on both sides, for heightened sensitivities to values like academic freedom, pastoral concern and many more. Indeed, the structure itself should become a barrier against arbitrary dismissal to the extent that it guides what theology is intended to do, namely, reflection on the data of revelation and the application of these understandings to the practice of life. Moreover, the presence of structured dialogue will help to shape the understanding of academic freedom on a given campus relative to theology. In some way, Catholic theology finds its base in the teaching of the magisterium. To make this relationship between Catholic bishops and Catholic theologians more visible even at the micro level of a given campus in a given diocese, will, I think, tend to increase the probability of theologians becoming more influential and more secure in their service to the church.

6 • Church, Academy, Law:
Personal Reflections

Charles E. Curran

This essay will reflect on the controversy between the Catholic University of America (CUA) and myself over the University's decision that, as a result of a definitive declaration from the Vatican Congregation for the Doctrine of the Faith, I could no longer teach Catholic theology at the Catholic University. In my analysis I will concentrate especially on the academic and legal aspects of the case. The analysis will avoid any attempt to reargue the case or to question the motives of anyone involved. This essay will assume that both parties acted to protect and preserve the values that they thought were threatened in this case. My purpose is threefold: to point out what happened, to interpret how and why the parties involved made the moves they did in the development of the case, and to look backward and forward from the present perspective. The final section will reflect especially on the broader question of academic freedom in American Catholic higher education.

The fundamental significance of the case must be seen in the light of three contexts: recent developments in Roman Catholicism, in American Catholic higher education, and in the self-understanding of the Catholic University of America. Within the church context, great changes occurred in Roman Catholicism after the Second Vatican Council (1962–1965), but some retrenchment on the part of church authorities has taken place in the last few years. In the late 1960s, Catholic higher education in general changed dramatically with its acceptance of academic freedom and institutional autonomy and with the establishment of lay-dominated boards of trustees that were no longer controlled by the sponsoring religious body.[1]

The Catholic University of America made similar striking changes in the late 1960s and early 1970s, precipitated and illustrated by two events.[2] In 1967 a university-wide strike closed the university, and the trustees then rescinded their decision not to renew my contract and give me a promotion as had been proposed by the requisite faculty and academic bodies. Prodding from the accrediting association and the experience of the strike occasioned the restructuring of CUA and its board of trustees to bring the institution into line with American standards.[3] In 1968 I acted as the spokesperson for 20 Catholic University professors and almost 600 other Catholic scholars in claiming that one could dissent in theory and in practice from the condemnation of artificial contraception in the papal encyclical *Humanae Vitae* and still be loyal a Roman Catholic. The trustees finally accepted, with regard to its academic propriety, the judgment of a faculty inquiry committee and of the academic senate that the subject professors had not violated their responsibilities as Catholic theologians by their declarations and actions in dissenting from one of the conclusions of the papal encyclical.[4] Most people thought that the recent changes in the university structure and the acceptance of this theological dissent proved that academic freedom was alive and well at Catholic University.

WHAT ACTUALLY HAPPENED?

One must be very clear about exactly what happened at the Catholic University in the present controversy. The impression is often given that what occurred affected only the ecclesiastical faculties (which will be explained later) and did not affect the whole university. Such an impression is wrong. The board of trustees decided as a matter of religious conviction and canon law that I could not teach Catholic theology anywhere at Catholic University.[5] I was removed from teaching in my area of competency without a judgment made in the first instance by peers that I was not competent.

External sources concluded that CUA as a whole violated the principles of academic freedom and institutional autonomy in my case. In the legal case in the Superior Court of the District of Columbia, Judge Frederick H. Weisberg decided in favor of the Catholic University; CUA had not violated its contractual obligations to me. However, to win its case the University had to admit that academic freedom does not exist at Catholic University. According to Judge Weisberg's decision, "nothing in its contract with Professor Curran or any other faculty member promises that it will always come down on the side of academic freedom."[6]

The American Association of University Professors (AAUP) censured Catholic University because of its actions.[7] The lengthy report of the AAUP investigating committee concluded that in the case of Professor Curran "the administration and the board of trustees of the Catholic University of America for all practical purposes deprived him of his tenure without due process and without adequate cause . . . [and] violated Professor Curran's academic freedom."[8]

One must be acquainted with the facts in the case to understand what truly happened. However, herein lies a problem. From an epistemological perspective I have to admit that pure objective facts do not exist, for the individuals concerned are always interpreting the facts. The experience of the this case, both with an academic hearing and with a long legal case and trial, proves that both sides could not agree on the facts. Recognizing the limitations and problems involved, I will strive for objectivity.

On 18 August 1986, Archbishop James A. Hickey, the chancellor of Catholic University, handed me a letter from Cardinal Joseph Ratzinger, the perfect of the Vatican Congregation for the Doctrine of the Faith, which informed me that I could "no longer be considered suitable nor eligible to exercise the function of a Professor of Catholic Theology." This declaration, which Ratzinger elsewhere referred to as a "definitive judgment," was approved by the pope. This declaration culminated an investigation of my writings that I was first informed about in the summer of 1979. At the same time Archbishop Hickey, in his position as chancellor of Catholic University, gave me a letter informing me that he was initiating the process for the withdrawal of my canonical mission. I had to respond by 1 September if I wanted to avail myself of the due process hearing guaranteed to me.[9]

To understand this proposed action fully and to interpret properly the whole case, one must be familiar with the structure of Catholic University.[10] In this very structure one sees the tension between being a *university* in the American understanding of the term and being a *Catholic* university. On the one hand, in 1887 Pope Leo XIII approved the foundation of Catholic University, and two years later he approved the statutes of the institution and endowed it with the rights proper to a lawfully constructed university in accord with Catholic canon law. Thus in this suit, Catholic University claimed that it is a juridical person in Catholic canon law and a pontifical university. Likewise, CUA has a special relationship with the bishops of the United States.

However, in 1887 Catholic University was also incorporated in the District of Columbia as an institution of learning with the rank of a university. In 1964 Catholic University opted to accept the provisions of the District of Columbia Nonprofit Corporation Act as an educational institution. Since 1900 Catholic University has been a member of the prestigious Association of American Universities and has been accredited by the Middle States Association of Colleges and Schools since the beginning of this association in 1921.

The current bylaws of the University place "ultimate responsibility for governance and sole responsibility for fiscal affairs of the University" in a board of trustees. At the present time, the board of trustees has 40 elected members equally divided between clerics and laypeople. Sixteen of the clerical members shall be members of the National Conference of Catholic Bishops, and cardinals who are diocesan bishops will normally be clerical members of the board of trustees. The bylaws also recognize that the Archbishop of Washington will be chancellor of the University and "shall serve as a liaison between the University and the National Conference of Catholic Bishops, as well as between the University and the Holy See."[11]

Catholic University also has three ecclesiastical faculties, or what American terminology would call departments (canon law, philosophy and theology) that are governed by a set of Canonical Statutes that have been approved by the Vatican in accordance with the norms proposed in official church documents.[12] According to these applicable norms, those Catholics teaching disciplines relating to faith and morals need from the chancellor a canonical mission to teach in the name of the church. The chancellor may withdraw the canonical mission only for the most serious reasons, and the faculty member may request the procedures for due process which *mutatis mutandis* are the same procedures used for the dismissal for cause of a tenured faculty member (Canonical Statutes V, 8). However, these faculties share the aims and goals of the entire University (II, 1 and 2). The chancellor is to "protect the doctrine and discipline of the church ... in accord with recognized academic procedures" (III, 7 g). These norms and practices concerning appointments to the faculties are "intended to assure fidelity to the revealing Word of God as it is transmitted by tradition and interpreted and safeguarded by the magisterium of the Church and to safeguard academic freedom" (V, 11). These canonical statutes came into effect in 1981.

"These Faculties, however, are not exclusively ecclesiastical; they also have other academic programs which do not have canonical effects and to which these Statutes do not apply" (I, 1). I was a member of the department of theology which, according to these statutes, "has a pontifical faculty." The heading of the statutes dealing with theology reads "Statutes of the Pontifical Degrees Program of the Department of Theology." I maintained in a letter to university authorities in 1981 and throughout the case that these statutes did not apply to me since they were unilaterally imposed by the University *after* my tenure contract was entered into in 1970.

All recognized that the canonical statutes were compromise documents. We as faculty insisted that the protection of academic freedom be written into the canonical statutes and that the ecclesiastical faculties be seen as integral parts of the university. However, the chancellor insisted that canonical mission be incorporated into the statutes and that his function of protecting the doctrine and discipline of the church be spelled out. The ambiguity of the statutes enabled everyone to live with them until the crunch came.

My first decision was whether or not to accept the due process procedures to defend myself against the chancellor's move to take away my canonical mission. I maintained that I had never received a canonical mission and did not need one since the new canonical statutes did not apply to me. Without waiving my rights in this matter, I agreed to accept the due process procedure as the way to get a hearing on the case. In retrospect, much time and effort would have been saved if I had simply conceded the issue of canonical mission and retained my claims as a tenured faculty member.

My position before the faculty hearing committee emphasized the academic freedom aspects of the case.[13] Academic freedom as accepted in the American academy means that a tenured professor can be dismissed for cause only after a judgment in the first instance by faculty peers about one's incompetence. The final decision is made by the governing board of the institution on the basis of this record. I based my position on two established principles: first, the protection of academic freedom written into the ecclesiastical statutes; and second, the decision of the 1968 faculty inquiry committee in the case of the dissenting professors that if there were the requirement of canonical mission, it had to be understood in accordance with established American academic principles and procedures. In my understanding, the faculty committee had to make a judgment about my competency in order to take away my canonical mission. The declaration from the Vatican congregation could be rebutted by other academic evidence of my competency as a Catholic moral theologian.

The chancellor's position was straightforward. The canonical mission is given to teach in the name of the church. The highest authorities in the Roman Catholic church had concluded that I was neither suitable nor eligible to be a professor of Catholic theology. This definitive judgment alone constituted the most serious reasons required by the statutes to take away the canonical mission.

The committee did not enter into the question of my competency but ultimately assumed my competency. However, the faculty committee did not think that the Vatican declaration was the only reality to be considered in the case. The report of the faculty committee recognized the "potential conflict" between the jurisdiction of the church on the one hand and the institutional autonomy of the university and my tenure rights on the other hand. The committee concluded that the board of trustees could take away the canonical mission only if I remained a tenured faculty member at Catholic University teaching in my area of competence somewhere in the university.[14]

Both the chancellor and I disagreed with the committee report.[15] The committee accepted my competency as well as the American academic principles of institutional autonomy and academic freedom in the university as a whole but recognized that such principles do not exist in the ecclesiastical faculty of theology. I had spent my career at CUA in working for the compatibility of academic freedom and Catholic universities, including theology. Now, in my judgment, the committee had concluded that academic freedom did not exist in the faculty of theology. I said at the time I was 75 percent satisfied with the committee report.

The chancellor and the board of trustees had even greater reservations with the committee report. They claimed that the committee had exceeded its mandate in saying anything beyond the right to take away the canonical mission. Also the committee had not given sufficient attention to the wording of the Vatican declaration that I was neither suitable nor eligible to teach Catholic theology in general and not just on an ecclesiastical faculty.[16]

After the faculty committee report, I was willing to live with the conclusion of the committee and at least for a time accept a position teaching in my area of competency elsewhere in the university. The academic freedom of the Catholic University as a whole would be vindicated even though such protection did not exist in the ecclesiastical faculty of theology. Also, after the committee report I could not realistically expect to teach in the faculty of theology.

In the spring of 1988, however, it became clear that

the chancellor, the administration, and the board of trustees had a different position. In the light of the declaration from the congregation they were determined that I could not teach Catholic theology anywhere at Catholic University. They were willing to allow me to teach social ethics, but I would have to accept the Vatican declaration as binding on me and thus I could not teach Catholic theology. I was willing to be called a professor of social ethics, but I could not accept the Vatican declaration as binding on me without denying the principles of academic freedom. In his deposition for the civil suit, Archbishop Hickey testified that it had been this position from the very beginning that I could not teach Catholic theology anywhere at Catholic University. In this whole enterprise the chancellor was the principal and leading actor. The board of trustees and the administration ultimately supported him in this contention.

At its 2 June 1988 meeting, the board of trustees took its final action in my case. "The Board accepts the declaration of the Holy See as binding upon the University as a matter of canon law and religious conviction."

> "[A]ny assignment allowing Father Curran to exercise the function of a Professor of Catholic Theology despite the Holy See's declaration that he is ineligible to do so would be inconsistent with the University's special relationship with the Holy See, incompatible with the University's freely chosen Catholic character, and contrary to the obligations imposed on the University as a matter of canon law."[17]

It should be noted that the administration and trustees of CUA could have used other means and arguments to achieve their goal of making sure that I did not teach Catholic theology at Catholic University. One other approach was briefly tried in the spring of 1988 but was ultimately replaced by the argument from religious conviction and canon law. The faculty committee had concluded that my canonical mission could be taken away if I continued to teach in my area of competency, "namely, as a professor in the area of moral theology and/or ethics." At one point the administration maintained that it was following this faculty committee report by offering me a teaching position in social ethics insisting that I sign a statement saying I would not teach Catholic theology at Catholic University because of the Vatican declaration. Catholic University officials did not pursue this approach. Perhaps they realized that their argument here was quite weak. Perhaps they purposely wanted to make another point.

In the course of the legal suit, other arguments were proposed by the University such as the nonabsolute character of academic freedom or the different nature of academic freedom for Catholic theology. However, these were subsidiary arguments at best that were developed in a different context. The primary reason for the action taken by the University remained that found in the final decision of the board of trustees in my case. As a matter of canon law and religious conviction, they could not allow me to teach Catholic theology at the Catholic University of America.

WHY DID THE PARTIES ACT AS THEY DID?

My strategy was clear. I believed that CUA had accepted academic freedom and that this was part of my contract. According to the principles of academic freedom, I could be removed from my teaching position *only* on the basis of a judgment of incompetency made in the first instance by peers. Such a process had not been followed in my case. Since the trustees did not accept the faculty committee report, I went to the Superior Court of the District of Columbia to pursue my claim that the University had violated my contract.

In retrospect, on the basis of the declarations and actions taken by the administration and trustees, it is easy to figure out what their strategy was. They were convinced that for the good of the Catholic University of

America as they understood it, with its special relationship to the Holy See, that I could no longer teach Catholic theology there. To achieve their goal they had to consider the different forums in which the issues would be discussed and the different means that might be used to accomplish their purpose.

From the very beginning of the case, the chancellor and the trustees gave great significance to the legal forum. They knew that the New York firm of Cravath, Swaine, and Moore had offered to represent and defend me throughout all the aspects of the case on a *pro bono* basis. I was willing to go to court if necessary to vindicate what I felt were my contractual rights.

What was the best legal defense for their position? The strongest possible defense and the one that might prevent the case from ever going to court involved first amendment rights. As a Catholic institution, CUA had the first amendment right to be free from government interference of any kind in determining who could teach Catholic theology at the institution. Such a defense was behind the final statement made by the board of trustees on my case in June 1988. Catholic University took its action against me on the basis of canon law and religious conviction. CUA's action was thus protected by the first amendment from any scrutiny by the civil courts.

The goal of preventing my teaching theology at Catholic University and first amendment defense of it would create some problems for the trustees and administration that any prudent person would have to consider. The first problem area concerned the faculty committee. The strategy adopted by the trustees meant that they could not accept the faculty committee report. They remanded the report to the committee with their disagreements. From a statutory viewpoint, the chancellor and the trustees were not legally obligated to follow the report, but there was strong moral suasion. By not following the committee report, the trustees put themselves in opposition to the committee, but the committee could do nothing about it. From a strategical perspective, the trustees apparently thought that they could disagree with the report without causing disproportionate problems for themselves and the institution. The faculty as a whole would probably take no drastic action, but there would be some dissatisfaction and even resolutions from the academic senate. The trustees and administration were correct in their apparent judgment that faculty reaction would not cause too many problems in the long run.

The second problem area concerned the broader academic community and the standing of Catholic University in that community. The prudent actor had to decide what would be involved here and what risks the contemplated action would bring about.

From past experience, all concerned knew that the AAUP would follow the case very closely. The AAUP both works for the acceptance of the norms of academic freedom and institutional autonomy and, as a last resort, censures the institutions that violate these principles. The Catholic University officials had to know that if I were not allowed to teach in my area of competence without a due process hearing by faculty peers, the AAUP would probably censure Catholic University. The AAUP insists above all on the need to follow the requisite procedures and ordinarily does not enter into the validity of the judgments made in accord with the established procedures. A censure from AAUP was all but inevitable.

Another aspect of the academic forum involved the general standing and reputation of the institution within the academic world. Would Catholic University's reputation be so tarnished by accepting the Vatican declaration as binding that it would lose face in the academic world? A more tangible problem concerned the accreditation of the institution by the Middle States Association of Colleges and Schools. If Catholic University violated the principles of academic freedom and institutional autonomy, the institution might lose its accreditation. Such a loss of accreditation would constitute a grave threat to the survival of Catholic University as an American institution of higher learning.

Eligibility for government aid and grants raised another potential problem. Earlier Supreme Court rulings had declared that federal aid to certain Catholic colleges was constitutional because, unlike grammar schools and high schools, Catholic colleges did not proselytize and did accept academic freedom. Perhaps federal funding for Catholic University would be jeopardized by the position taken in my case.

In retrospect, the officials of Catholic University were willing to run all of these risks. Why? The simplest and most radical response to the question rests on what ethicists call a strict deontological approach. The officials were convinced in conscience that their understanding of Catholic University and their commitment to the Catholic Church called for them to take this action against me no matter what the consequences. Perhaps some did take this position, but others as prudent trustees and administrators would also have wanted to examine all the possible consequences of their action. In this interpretation, the actors concluded that the risks to Catholic University in the academic forum would not be that proportionately harmful to Catholic University.

Why did the risks in the academic forum not deter the Catholic University officials from taking the action they did? First of all, the academic interests were not the main concern of most of the decisionmakers. The evidence points to the fact that the primary actors were Archbishop James A. Hickey as the chancellor and the more senior cardinals and bishops on the board of trustees. None of these people had much association with the academic world and did not feel a true commitment to the principles of the American academy. They were and are primarily church persons. Their main source of advice did not come from academics but from civil lawyers who were involved from the very first moment in August 1986. The only person involved with any true academic experience was Father William J. Byron, S.J. the president. Thus the academic forum was not the primary concern or interest of the principal decision-makers. In addition, academic standing or reputation is a rather nebulous concept that is hard to pin down.

However, prudence would call for some discussion of the risks involved in the action taken. An AAUP censure would not be fatal to the institution. Other Catholic colleges and universities such as Marquette and Detroit have been censured by the AAUP and have not been greatly affected by it. Institutions would prefer to avoid such censures, but Catholic University could live with a censure from the AAUP. In fact, as noted earlier, the AAUP *did* censure Catholic University.

What about the threat of losing accreditation? A prudent and realistic judgment could conclude that Catholic University probably would not lose its accreditation. This action in my case was a single act involving one person and did not directly affect other faculty members. History points out the reluctance of the accrediting associations to take away accreditation. In 1966 St. John's University in Jamaica fired 32 faculty members including six with tenure without any due process, but the institution never lost its accreditation. One of my advisers compared the decision to take away accreditation with the decision to use the nuclear bomb on the part of so-called realistic politicians. People are and should be reluctant to use such ultimate weapons.

My advisers and I concluded very early on that CUA would probably not lose its accreditation over this issue. However, I was somewhat surprised that the accrediting evaluation team "differed on their perspectives of the issue of academic freedom at CUA in the light of the Curran affair."[18] In the end the committee report did not even slap the institutional wrists of CUA in this regard.

The loss of government aid and grants would definitely constitute a serious problem for the future of the University. Catholic University was represented in this case by Williams and Connolly, whose lawyers had been intimately involved in these cases and the discussions surrounding them. Such loss of funding could come about

only if someone sued Catholic University in court.
However, the university had a fallback position. The
president had told faculty members that, if necessary,
the University would separately incorporate the three
ecclesiastical faculties and perhaps all religious studies
on campus. These entities receive little or no government funding at this time. Such separate incorporation
would allow the church to maintain direct control over
these dapartments and schools without jeopardizing government aid to the rest of the institution. Again, the
academic concern of the standing of these separated
entities was not of primary importance for the decision-
makers. Academics in general and academics in the religious studies would be seriously concerned about such
a second-class categorization, but such concerns did not
greatly affect the trustees and their lawyers.

One must appreciate the risks that were run by the
Catholic University officials. They were unwilling to
accept and live with the position that I had lost my
canonical mission and could not teach in an ecclesiastical faculty, but I would teach social ethics in the
Department of Sociology. This would have included
academic contacts with theology students not in the ecclesiastical degree programs. If they had accepted such
an outcome, the Catholic University trustees would have
avoided opposing a faculty committee, an AAUP censure, any problem with academic reputation, and any fear
of losing major government aid and grants. At one time
in early April 1987 I thought that the administration and
trustees were willing to accept this position. However,
they did not.

RETROSPECT AND PROSPECT

Judge Frederick H. Weisberg issued his decision on
28 February 1989. I lost the case. The judge rejected the
first amendment defense and ruled that he had a right
to hear the case based on my contract with the Catho-

lic University of America, which is civilly incorporated in the District of Columbia. However, according to the decision, I was bound by the 1981 canonical statutes and hence had a canonical mission that was properly taken away. The University had no obligation to allow me to teach theology in the nonecclesiastical parts of the University since my tenure was to the Department of Theology. The court pointed out the ambivalence of Catholic University. It wanted to have it both ways in being a full-fledged American university and in having a unique and special relationship with the Holy See. "[N]othing in its contract with Professor Curran or any other faculty member promises that it will always come down on the side of academic freedom." The judge also declared that even if I had won the case, he would not have granted specific performance.[19]

The court did not accept my contention that I was never given a canonical mission and also was not bound by the canonical statutes of 1981, which added a substantial new element to my contract. More significantly, neither my contract nor any contract at the time of my tenure (1970–1971) included the guarantee of academic freedom. I had relied on many statements made by the academic senate and sent in the name of the University to official bodies such as the Middle States Association, but only those statements made by the board of trustees are part of the contract. As for specific performance, my lawyers had always known how difficult it would be to win specific performance in this kind of contract case.

As for the future, I cannot teach Catholic theology at Catholic University. A number of colleagues from Catholic institutions of higher learning have admitted that their institutions will not hire me. Apparently they are afraid of offending Rome, the American bishops, and some of their own supporters.[20] I have now found a very congenial academic home at Southern Methodist University as the Elizabeth Scurlock University Professor of Human Values.

Before going to SMU, however, I became embroiled in another academic freedom case at Auburn University. I had been offered and accepted the Goodwin-Philpott Eminent Scholar Chair in Religion at Auburn in April of 1990 with the understanding that this was a tenured position. However, James E. Martin, the president of Auburn, changed his mind and refused to give me tenure. The University Senate of Auburn censured President Martin "for violations of academic principles and policies as they relate to the issue of tenure for Professor Curran." Among the specifics was his being pressured by persons outside the tenure process, specifically certain members of the Auburn board of trustees, to influence unduly a tenure decision.[21]

I will probably never know accurately the full story of what transpired at Auburn. At various times the question of Catholic church involvement arose. I am convinced that Catholic church authorities and/or individual Catholics did not and could not alone block my tenure. However, it seems that the question would never have arisen unless Catholics first brought up the fact that I was controversial. Other people then used this fact to achieve their own purposes.

Back now to *Curran v. Catholic University*. Catholic University won the case, but the judge did not accept its first amendment defense. In retrospect, the University did not have to go as far as it did to prevent my teaching there. However, the insistence on religious conviction and canon law could have contributed to the judge's decision that contracts at CUA do not guarantee academic freedom for faculty. As for the future, CUA will have to live with the consequences of its declarations and actions. Only time will tell what the CUA faculty will be willing and able to accomplish and how the higher education community will react to what has occurred.

The case has not broken any new ground in the legal area. The court rejected the argument that the action of Catholic University was immune from court scrutiny because of its religious freedom. In my nonexpert opinion, religious freedom *should* protect certain actions of churches but *not* those institutions that are incorporated as institutions of higher education. Catholic University still might be vulnerable to a suit challenging its right to government aid and grants.

This case also has implications for Catholic higher education in the United States. The very core issue in this case has been the nature and identity of a Catholic university or college. Catholic University has some unique characteristics, certainly, but it still claims to be an American university.

Can what happened to me at Catholic University also happen at other Catholic institutions of higher learning? The answer is *yes*. The board of trustees at Catholic University, on the basis of its religious conviction, said that the Vatican declaration was binding on them. Boards of trustees at other Catholic institutions could make the same decision. Note that by making the decision based on its religious conviction and free choice, the board tried to defend its own autonomy. No one is telling the board what to do. Parenthetically this brings up a significant ambiguity in the concept of institutional autonomy in relation to academic freedom. Autonomy could be wrongly invoked to violate academic freedom. A board is not free to accept a position that violates the academic freedom of one of its professors.

The more precise question is whether the boards of other Catholic institutions of higher learning would as a matter of fact make the same decision as the Catholic University board. I have some doubts. The Catholic University board consists of 16 American bishops, including the most prestigious Catholic hierarchical leaders in the United States. On issues such as this one, the other members of the board tend to follow the lead of the cardinals and bishops. Depositions taken from two lay board members in my case corroborate this understanding.[22] Most other college and university boards probably have only one or at most a few bishops on the board. Many other board members would also have a strong commitment to the principles of academic freedom. I doubt if such boards would easily make the same kind of decision as the Catholic University board did.

The reaction of the leadership of the mainstream of Catholic higher education in the United States to my case has been fascinating. This group has strongly supported academic freedom for Catholic higher education. In response to a reporter's question about the reaction of such persons to my case, I replied that they are either like Pilate or Nicodemus. They have either washed their hands and had nothing to do with the case, or they have come by night to tell me of their distress. To my knowledge, none of these leaders explicitly and publicly defended Catholic University, but none of them has explicitly and squarely condemned Catholic University. Some have pointed out—in my judgment erroneously—that what happened to me could occur at Catholic University because it is a pontifical university, but it could not happen at their institutions.[23]

Rodger Van Allen, a professor at Villanova University who has written on academic freedom issues and is a former president of the College Theology Society, pointed out early on in my controversy that the best thing for Catholic higher education would be if a major Catholic University hired me.[24] However, as Richard McBrien and Richard McCormick, two distinguished theologians from Notre Dame University, have shown, this did not happen despite some attempts by faculty of these institutions. "We regard this exclusion as a continuing complicity in the original injustice done to Father Curran and as harmful, not only to him, but also to Catholic higher education in this country and to the church."[25]

The issue of academic freedom for Catholic higher education in the United States is still up in the air. On 26 September 1990, Pope John Paul II issued *Ex Corde Ecclesiae*, an apostolic constitution on Catholic universities that culminated 20 years of conversations and negotiations.[26] The leadership of the mainstream of

Catholic higher education in the United States (e.g., the presidents of Catholic University, Fordham and Notre Dame, as well as the executive secretary of the Association of Catholic Colleges and Universities) warmly received the document.[27] *America* editorialized: "The constitution also unequivocally affirms two basic qualities that must be possessed by any school aspiring to be a university: institutional autonomy and academic freedom."[28] On the other hand, Archbishop Rembert Weakland said about this constitution and subsequent events: "I'm sure if I were president of any Catholic university, I'd be nervous at this point. I'd want some clarifications."[29] I, too, have expressed grave reservations about the constitution.[30]

Such a difference in evaluation by people generally committed to the principles and practices of academic freedom for Catholic higher education points up the ambiguities in the apostolic constitution. Those warmly accepting the document point out that this new constitution incorporates important changes from the earlier drafts. The Vatican congregation listened to and often accepted the comments of Catholic higher educators in the United States. In addition, the pope insists that "a Catholic University is distinguished by its free search for the whole truth about nature, man, and God" (n. 4). Institutional autonomy and academic freedom are mentioned and defended (n. 12). Theology is a legitimate academic discipline, and theologians enjoy academic freedom so long as they are faithful to theology's principles and methods (n. 29).

However, there exists another position—and probably even a stronger and more fundamental one—in the document that limits institutional autonomy and academic freedom. The institutional fidelity of the university to the church requires an adherence to the teaching authority of the church in matters of faith and morals (n. 27). Bishops are not external agents to the university but participate in the life of Catholic institutions of higher learning (n. 28). Academic freedom is limited by the "confines of the truth and the common good" (n. 29). Those who teach theological disciplines in these institutions must have a mandate from the competent ecclesiastical authority (Part II, a. 3).

My personal experience makes me very wary of such ambiguous documents. I had thought that the 1981 canonical statutes for the pontifical faculties of the Catholic University could be lived with because they contained a strong defense of academic freedom and academic procedures. However, such statements were relativized by the other statements in the document. One can only logically conclude that this present document and its official interpreters, in a conflict situation, would not come down on the side of academic freedom.

Catholic higher education leaders in the United States rightly point to the document's insistence that Catholic universities do not have to be established officially by church authorities or by a public juridical person in the church, thus making them institutionally subordinate to the church authorities (Part II, a. 3). However, such institutions can call themselves Catholic only with the consent of the competent ecclesiastical authority (Part II, a. 3). Such Catholic institutions that do not have a direct juridical tie to the church (this includes the vast majority of those in the United States) "with the agreement of the local ecclesiastical Authority, will make their own the General Norms and their local and regional applications internalizing them into their governing documents, and, as far as possible, will conform their existing Statutes both to these General Norms and to their applications" (Part II, a. 1–3). Also these norms must take into account the statutes of each university or institute, and, as far as possible and appropriate, civil law (Part II, a. 1–2).

Those supporters of academic freedom for Catholic higher education who warmly receive the constitution put heavy emphasis on these provisions. The norms for each country are to be drawn up locally and to recognize existing statutes, customs and—even as far as possible and appropriate—civil law. There is nothing in the constitution that would prohibit Catholic institutions of higher learning in the United States from continuing to function as they have done in the immediate past. Adaptation to local conditions, customs and civil law is acceptable. In the past, the American Catholic bishops have supported the leaders of Catholic higher education in their insistence on academic freedom and institutional autonomy for these schools.

However, there might be some problems. First of all, there is now an official document that does not recognize *full* academic freedom and institutional autonomy. Second, in the last few years a good number of Catholic bishops in the United States have come out *against* full academic freedom.[31] In these more conservative days of contemporary American Catholicism, it will be much more difficult for the American Catholic bishops as a whole to accept and defend academic freedom. Supporters of academic freedom for Catholic higher education should be worried and concerned.

In these present personal reflections, I have accepted the good will and good intentions of those who are in favor of academic freedom as well as those who oppose academic freedom and institutional autonomy for the Catholic institutions of higher learning. My own personal experience and reflection on the board range of recent events lead me to conclude that the issue is far from settled. Supporters of academic freedom should be worried and work in theory and in practice to prove that academic freedom is good for Catholic higher education and ultimately for the church itself.[32]

7 • Symmetry Between Academic Freedom and a Catholic University

John E. Murray, Jr.

The first systematic definition of academic freedom appeared in 1915 when a committee of professors announced the General Report of the committee on Academic Freedom and Academic Tenure at the first annual meeting of the American Association of University Professors (AAUP). The report contained a "Declaration of Principles" that was largely influenced by the experience in German universities. In the latter part of the nineteenth century, thousands of American college graduates had gone to Germany for graduate work and returned with the conviction that American universities should adopt the German concept of academic freedom.[1] The original statement was refined in 1925, and further studies generated the 1940 Statement of Principles on Academic

Freedom and Tenure that has been endorsed by hundreds of learned societies. That statement remains unchanged notwithstanding interpretive comments added in 1969.

The AAUP statement begins with the principle that, "[T]he common good depends upon the free search for truth and its free exposition" and academic freedom is essential to these purposes. Thus, the teacher must have full freedom in research and the publication of results, though research for pecuniary gain must be based upon an understanding with the institution. Teachers are entitled to freedom in the classroom in discussing their subjects but they should be carefull to avoid introducing controversial matter having no relation to their subjects. When teachers speak in the capacity of a citizen, they must be free from institutional censorship or discipline, but their special position as a member of a learned profession and officer of an educational institution imposes special obligations, i.e., they must remember that the public may judge their profession and their institutions by their utterances. They should, therefore, at all times be accurate, exercise appropriate restraint, show respect for the opinions of others and make every effort to indicate that they are not institutional spokespersons.[2] This statement of academic freedom is often characterized as "authoritative."[3] The number of institutions and societies that have incorporated it lend support to this characterization.

Yet, the statement could hardly be called comprehensive or without difficulty in application. Indeed, in a recent article, the president and associate counsel for AAUP state that questions regularly arise concerning the meaning of academic freedom. They say, "The very core of the doctrine remains confused. . . ."[4] There are, of course numerous definitions of academic freedom. One historian has recently suggested major differences between the "professional" and "constitutional" definitions, noting that American courts had not mentioned the concept prior to the middle of this century.[5] The meaning of "academic freedom," like other abstract concepts, will continue to evolve and become more comprehensive only as it is applied in myriad situations. With the exception that the statement refers only to him rather than him or her, as a general statement of the concept, the AAUP statement is perfectly acceptable.

Like any other freedom, academic freedom is said to be limited. These "limitations" may take on many forms beyond the express limitations in the AAUP statement. A school or department within any university will have its favors and frowns. A department committed to the Harvard School of economics will not accept a major thrust toward the Chicago School. Certain departments of philosophy or psychology will reject a phenomenological approach while phenomenologists have little respect for behaviorist or Freudian psychology. Family history will receive a different treatment at Stanford from its treatment at Yale. Religious studies will be treated as a discipline in certain universities and ignored or treated harshly in other universities. Deconstructionist approaches in various disciplines will be rejected in some departments or schools while in others that approach will constitute a *sine qua non* to any association with the school or department. Advancement in certain universities will depend exclusively upon scholarship while others will insist upon a clear manifestation of highly effective teaching as well as scholarship.

Within any discipline, the individual scholar is also limited by his or her ignorance of other disciplines that impinge upon research. In my own discipline of law, it is increasingly important to be aware of developments in philosophy, economics, history, sociology and other relevant dimensions. Securing collegial assistance in dealing with these important dimensions will be qualitatively different from one university to another.

Beyond these and other endemic limitations on academic freedom, there is a pervasive limitation that one often discovers in secular universities. It is an orthodoxy that permeates virtually any department or school. The ordinary religion of the secular university is, at best, value neutrality or relativism[6] which often descends to a concerted assault on values. We live in an age of reductionism, and one philosopher has recently described the concerted assault of the reductionists as follows:

> Religious attachment involves no contact with the divine, and is merely a way of coping with our fears, a projection of our hopes or infantile psychology (views associated with Hume and Freud); Social and political principles, despite their claim to validity, are ideological superstructure, generated and maintained by needs for rationalization of ruling groups or hierarchical structures, or [they] are a function of social position (Marx, Mannheim). [Such principles may also be viewed as] summary rules of thumb for social and wealth maximization (the 'economic analysis of law'). The individual person is buffeted and directed by unconscious repressed desires, his rational reasons are merely rationalizations, his valuable activitieś, literary and artistic, merely redirections of other energy, viewed as baser, now sublimated (Freud). Our voluntary behavior and major life plans are the playing out of patterns and conflicts established in early childhood (Freud) or are under the control of external stimuli, past history of reinforcement and current drive state (Pavlov, Watson, Hull [and] Skinner), of innate desires instilled in the evolutionary process and serving (at least once upon a time) our inclusive fitness (the literature of sociobiology), or of biochemical and electrical activity in our brain and current hormone balances (Olds [and] Delgado). [We can also explain cultural patterns and personal actions and relationships such as marriage, religious attendance, childbearing, friendship and suicide not by the reasons people offer, but by] the energetic requirements and needs of society (Harris) or by more general self-interested economic calculations (Becker), or other calculations of balance of benefit.[7]

Not all of these theories can be true. That, however, does not matter to the reductionist whose sole and exclusive purpose is devaluation, allowing us all to share in the

growing consciousness of lower and lower self-esteem.
I agree with the same philosopher who suggests that,
"Reductionism is not simply a theoretical mistake, it is
moral failing."[8]

To speak, however, of morals, apart from predilection,
is clearly erroneous, according to the orthodoxy. This
problem is illustrated most recently by the charge of the
president of Harvard University, Derek Bok. Bok claims
that Harvard and other secular universities have failed
to foster the moral growth of their students. Students
are leaving the universities bewildered and confused
because they are convinced that one view of morality
is necessarily equal to any other. Morality must be a
matter of opinion. Bok suggests that the university community may

> feel awkward in [discussing ethical issues]. Some believe
> that such talk will seem soft and sentimental in an
> atmosphere that appears to value intellectual toughness
> and close analysis. Others worry that they will be thought
> to be pompous and overbearing. At bottom, many may
> harbor a secret fear that once they start discussing ethical
> issues openly, they will reach conclusions that force them
> into troubling reassessments of their lives and future ca-
> reers.[9]

It is anything but remarkable that the study of morality would be ignored in an atmosphere of relativism, reductionism and nihilism. Bok complains that just two
years ago, the only available teacher of medical ethics
at the Harvard Medical School was a graduate student.
In such an atmosphere, the pursuit of a career pattern
based upon the objective existence of values and morality, much less religion, does not augur great success. If
the president wants morality taught in such a university, the followers of the orthodoxy may very well respond, "Whose morality? Shall it be the president's
personal view?"

When President Robert Maynard Hutchins of the University of Chicago delivered lectures[10] suggesting meta-

physics to be the highest, first and universal science, the response of John Dewey was clear:

> I would not intimate that the author has any sympathy with fascism. But basically his idea as to the proper course to be taken is akin to the distrust of freedom and the consequent appeal to some fixed authority that is now overrunning the world.... Doubtless such may be said for selecting Aristotle and Saint Thomas as competent promulgators of first truths. But it took the authority of a powerful ecclesiastical organization to secure their wide recognition. Others may prefer Hegel, or Karl Marx, or even Mussolini as the seers of first truths; and there are those who prefer Nazism. As far as I can see President Hutchins has completely evaded the problem of who is to determine the definite truths that constitute the hierarchy.[11]

As soon as scholars speak of first principles or objective values, they may be viewed as distrusting freedom, as authoritarian, or even as a fascist. One might wonder whether John Dewey subscribed to the AAUP admonition to be accurate, to respect the opinions of others and to pusue appropriate restraint. There is an even darker suspicion of anyone who suggests any credence of the views of Aquinas. When Hutchins's friend and colleague, Mortimer Adler, announced his adherence to Thomism, and Hutchins insisted upon principles that sounded more than reminiscent of Thomism, Adler tells us, "Rumors of all sorts were rife at the University of Chicago—that Bob Hutchins and I had been secretly baptized, that we had been seen on our knees at the altar rail of the Catholic church near the university campus."[12]

Professor Lon Fuller of the Harvard Law School spent much of his life insisting on the inseparability of the *is* and the *ought*, warring against the dominant English and American legal philosophy of the twentieth century, logical positivism, which insisted upon a rigid separation of that which *is* from that which *ought to be*. The positivists insisted that what one ought to do is a matter of morality, which must be a matter of opinion. The influence of David Hume was complete. When Fuller's book, *The Morality of Law*,[13] developed an inner morality of law and specified eight principles that must be met if any pronouncement should be given the effect of law, his position was ridiculed by Ronald Dworkin, as Dworkin defended the leading exponent of positivism, H. L. A. Hart of Oxford.[14] Now logical positivism is dead, though the law schools are only belatedly beginning to surrender the last vestige of this approach, and Dworkin now spends his time attacking Hart. Fuller has been heralded by former detractors since his death. Unfortunately, Fuller and others have been replaced at the Harvard Law School with so-called Critical Legal Scholars who pronounce an extreme form of deconstruction and systematically violate the principle that you do not reject a theory until a better theory is available.[15] Meanwhile, an Oxford Fellow has recently produced a superior treatment of natural law in the Thomistic tradition which clearly overcomes the vested, traditionally mistaken views of that brilliant treatment of legal philosophy.[16] The notion, however, that only nonevaluative criteria can be genuine knowledge pervades higher education in America.

This is the ambience in which academic freedom is heralded. In this ambience, by definition, truth cannot be discovered, much less advanced, because truth beyond the natural sciences does not exist. It is the great paradox of the secular university that we cannot discern the good life which necessarily includes a good called knowledge. The Catholic university rejects relativism, nihilism and the noncognitive ethics that surround it. It rejects reductionism. It rejects any notion that it is impossible to understand what is good. It accepts the intellectual virtues as real. It is willing to discuss what a person ought to do because it is committed to the view that what ought to be done to achieve the good life, the full life, can be known. Catholic universities are classical universities because they see their purpose as maximizing those conditions necessary for the complete development of each member of the university community. We do not pretend to have the immediate or final solution to every complex moral or ethical dilemma. We recognize that these questions are not easily answered. The difference is that we believe truth exists. We will pursue any argument, any analysis, and any knowledge in our quest for truth. As St. Augustine said, "Whatever is true is ours." We are compelled to search for truth because a Catholic university is a faith community, and our faith teaches us that God is perfect truth. There can be no incompatibility between our faith and reason because we have a sophisticated understanding of the fact that reason serves faith and faith aids reason. Unlike the relativists and reductionist, we understand why the act of faith is the most rational af all acts. There can be no conflict between faith and reason, both of which are subservient to truth, which is the first loyalty of the mind. In a Catholic university, therefore, we are compelled to seek truth unfettered by any predilection.

A Catholic university has a vision of university education. Many secular universities do not have a different vision; they have no vision at all of what an educated human being ought to be. They shrink from any evaluative criteria even with respect to curricular design. Students must not be told what courses to take, even at the start of their university journey. This view is totally consistent with relativism, reductionism and nihilism because it avoids telling individuals what they ought to do. It is, however, totally inconsistent with any rational concept of a university, which should recognize the critical importance of the humanities as well as other indispensable dimensions for the educated person.

A recent National Endowment for the Humanities survey reports that 78 percent of the nation's colleges and universities allow students to graduate without one course in the history of Western civilization, and 38 percent require no course in history of any kind. In 45 percent of our colleges and universities, students need take no course in American or English literature, and

77 percent require no foreign language. There is no
mathematics requirement in 41 percent of our schools,
and 33 percent require no course in the natural or physical sciences. By insisting that every student be exposed
to these and other critical dimensions, Duquesne University announces its vision of university education. By
including the critical dimension of theology, Duquesne
not only pursues its Catholic inspiration, but reinforces
its commitment to essential university education. We
do not apologize for a core curriculum that requires all
of the classic dimensions including religious studies.
Rather, we assert that this kind of university education
is quintessential to the advancement of truth. If students
are only aware of the views of David Hume, Bertrand
Russell or John Paul Sartre and have never heard of
Aristotle or Aquinas, it will be difficult for those students to pursue truth. If students have never been exposed to classical literature and history as well as
economics or given a fundamental appreciation of mathematics and science, the contribution of those students
to society will be severely limited. Regardless of the
student's belief, if he or she is totally unaware of the
spiritual dimension, the university has abdicated its
responsibility in establishing those conditions necessary
for the complete development of the student.

   Much of the discussion of academic freedom in Catholic universities is apologetic in tone. Relativism and
reductionism have invaded Catholic universities with
the insidious suggestion that because these universities
have announced their particular vision, they have
necessarily limited academic freedom. One can still hear
the view that the phrase "Catholic university" is an
oxymoron, and the same characterization is applied to
"Catholic intellectual." This view is particularly seen in
questions concerning theology. Two well-known theologians, Father Richard McBrien and Father Charles Curran exemplify this controversy. McBrien insists that, "If
[church-related] institutions want their colleges and
universities 'identified and accredited as institutions of

higher education,' they have to honor and abide by the principles of 'secular' academic freedom—as they stand, not in some unrecognizable caricature."[17] As practiced in many American universities, however, "academic freedom" "as it stands" is a perversion of the AAUP statement on academic freedom. That statement insists that the dominant purpose of academic freedom is the advancement of truth. The relativism, reductionism and nihilism of the orthodoxy in American higher education insists that truth does not exist in anything other than the natural sciences, where it is extremely limited.

As for the discipline of theology, if it were recognized as a discipline, the kind of limitations that McBrien expressly accepts in a Catholic university would be anathema to academic freedom as practiced in a secular university. He suggests that, "[T]he academic freedom of the Catholic theologian is limited by revelation and the teaching authority of the church. If a theologian wishes to be identified and recognized as a Catholic theologian, he or she cannot at the same time reject . . . any doctrinally positive [pronouncements of the church]."[18] Curran also seeks Catholic university identity with the mainstream of academic freedom. But, he recently insisted that, "The hierarchical teaching office of the pope and bishops comes with their Church position. The office is subject to the word of God and the truth according to the constitution on Divine Revelation of Vatican II. This teaching authority, with the help of the Holy Spirit, discerns the truth and the word of God."[19] He further insists that "a Catholic theologian [must] theologize within the sources and parameters of the Catholic faith," and if he fails in this mandate, he may be dismissed for incompetency.[20] Specifically, he states, "Academic peers could rightly judge incompetent a Catholic theologian who does not believe in Jesus or does not accept a role for the Pope in the Church."[21]

This view has been denounced by secular proponents of academic freedom as an absurd attempt to reconcile a limitation on the concept of academic freedom.[22] With unassailable logic, they suggest that a theologian who does not believe in Jesus or does not accept a role for the pope in the church may be competent. This theologian is not, however, a *Catholic* theologian, just as an economist who repudiates a free market theory may be perfectly competent but is not a member of the Chicago School. When McBrien and Curran insist that Catholic theologians must be limited in their academic freedom, they find no agreement with this view from secular proponents of academic freedom—again, that same academic freedom that McBrien insists Catholic universities must accept if they are to be true universities.

Let me use McBrien/Curran terminology to suggest what I see as their particular concerns. They are troubled, not by adherence to the teachings of the church that are "central" to the faith, but by compelled adherence to "distant" teachings.[23] Those teachings that are "central" are sometimes called "infallible" or "definitive" while the "distant" teachings are labeled "fallible" or "non-definitive."[24] Curran suggests that "the amount of deference [the theologian must give to official hierarchical teaching] depends on the level of the official hierarchical teaching,"[25] i.e., whether it is "central" (infallible) or "distant" (noninfallible). McBrien unequivocally asserts that the bishops should not make final judgments on these "distant" or noninfallible teachings.[26]

Though the analogy is imperfect, it has been suggested that the magisterium be likened to the United States Supreme Court by American Catholic theologians. The Supreme Court is final because a final arbiter is essential in any society. Finality is a very high value. Mr. Justice Jackson said, "we are not final because we are infallible; we are infallible because we are final." McBrien rejects this analogy because he believes that bishops are not professionally trained and active theologians, whereas Supreme Court justices are professionally trained and professionally active jurists.[27] He adds, "The fact that some few bishops may have earned a theological doctorate 20 or 30 years ago does not change this point.

Almost none of them was ever professionally active in teaching, in professional societies, or through publications in scholarly journals or books."[28]

This notion of the scholarship or education of Supreme Court Justices is not accurate. There is no member of the United States Supreme Court who ever earned a doctorate in constitutional law. Like other lawyers, they attended law school and took one course in Constitutional law, never exceeding six credits, 30 years ago. Their professional lives rarely presented them with a constitutional law question. The constitutional law scholars of America are not on the Supreme Court of the United States; they are in the law schools. The scholars know that members of the Supreme Court are not constitutional law scholars. In fact, the only recent constitutional law scholar who was considered for that court was rejected because of his scholarship. Notwithstanding inevitable criticism of constitutional interpretations in every case by at least some scholars, those same scholars have a much higher regard for the process and finality of decision making by the Supreme Court than McBrien seems to argue for the magisterium. Constitutional law scholars understand the overriding necessity for certainly, stability and finality in any normative process. Changes in the interpretation of the Constitution or other federal statutes have occured almost imperceptibly to the average person. The Supreme Court and constitutional scholars recognize that abrupt reversals war against the high values of certainty and stability which are essential to any normative system. The constitutional law scholars will be quick to tell students that a particular activity is unconstitutional because of a decision of the Court, whether or not the scholar happens to agree with that decision. Constitutional law scholars have complete respect for the decision-making process and finality of decision. We should recall Curran's statement that the hierarchical teaching office, with the help of the Holy Spirit, discerns the truth and the word of God. The Supreme Court of the United States makes no such claim for its decision-making process. Yet, it is perceived to be, and is, final. There is no dearth of constitutional law scholarship, much of which slowly finds its way into opinions of Supreme Court Justices, just as the views of many Catholic theologians are eventually regarded as the living tradition of Catholicism through the magisterium which must preserve the values of certainty and stability as the official promulgator of Catholic doctrine. It must, therefore, be final. Non-Catholic legal scholars who manifest sympathy for Curran's views are quick to emphasize the necessity of recognizing the magisterium as the final authority.[29]

When one devotes a lifetime to scholarship, it is inevitable that he or she becomes opinionated and impatient with other views. Over many years of research and scholarship in my discipline, I have developed certain analytical constructs to which I now cling, and I do not suffer other views gladly. Moreover, the tone of my published scholarship displays a distinct proclivity toward stridency. It is difficult for me to adhere strictly to the AAUP admonition to state my views with appropriate restraint and respect for the opinions of others. I suspect that a number of my colleagues in other disciplines suffer from this malady. For example, McBrien says that the bishops are developing a "party line" concerning academic freedom in Catholic universities.[30] Another theologian casts aside the last scintilla of restraint for the opinions of others by suggesting that the bishops seek "hierarchical control of Catholic universities."[31] This is even more strident than my writing. I try to remember that my scholarship is a small part of the total contribution made by all of the scholars in my discipline. Since my scholarship often suggests changes in normative concepts, I also recognize that the assimilation process will require long periods and that I may not be here to feel the satisfaction of some of my work becoming the final teaching in my discipline. There is even frustration in learning that one's contributions have been accepted. By the time they have been accepted, I may believe that they are passe since I have since refined my analysis and look upon the adoption of my own work as reflecting a primitive understanding. A scholar who finds these restraints unacceptably frustrating will be hard pressed to continue the lonely and difficult process of scholarship.

I am troubled by any suggestion that academic freedom can be limited by any external force in any discipline, including theology. Even though some insist that the AAUP statement on Academic Freedom itself contains limitations, this characterization is misleading. For example, the AAUP concern that teachers not introduce controversial matter into their teaching that is not related to their subject matter speaks not to academic freedom but to relevancy and competency. The AAUP is also concerned that teachers, as citizens, should remember that the public may judge their profession and institutions by their utterances and, therefore, these utterances should always be accurate, should show respect for the opinion of others and clearly indicate that the teacher is not an institutional spokesperson. This speaks not to academic freedom but to prudence.

In any discipline, teachers should be prudent in the classroom. The teacher of freshman economics who begins the first class with the startling pronouncement that macroeconomics is a fallacy and all of the theory to be presented in this course on that subject is a snare and a delusion cannot possibly believe that the students will understand. These students are not ready to discuss this assertion intelligently. This leader may produce undisciplined followers who simply parrot these conclusions. This teacher is not, however, providing education for the students. The same statement could be addressed to another scholar or Ph.D. candidate in economics who would have reason to understand the views of this scholar. Intermediate or advanced French should not be attempted until the student has completed an introduction to that subject. My conversations with scholars in my discipline may appear highly controversial and even shocking to the untutored. It is essential, however, to explore the frontiers of my discipline, and the interaction with other scholars in a critically important component of the effort. They are not shocked by my views because they enjoy a comprehensive understanding of the discipline and discern my thrusts as extentions of that discipline.

Prudent judgments are particularly important in attempting to bring scholarly views to the public. We live in the era of the 30-second bite—the headline statement that often conceals truth. The Mid-East scholar is sought out to react to the latest developments in Iran or Lebanon. The legal scholar is asked to sum up his analysis of the most recent voluminous United States Supreme Court opinion dealing with a controversial topic. The theologian is asked to provide a comprehensive view of sexual morality. These scholars are supposed to condense a lifetime of scholarship into a maximum of 30 seconds to provide certain answers to the current crisis. Their efforts to provide thoughtful, fundamentals analyses are constantly frustrated by the interviewer who deplores long responses. The AAUP statement requires the scholar to be accurate in such public pronouncements, but the last fig leaf of accuracy may wind up on the cutting room floor of the television studio. The goal is anything but a scholarly exchange. The scholar has to be particularly careful to avoid the blinding light of publicity which may seem attractive when compared to the hermitical existence of genuine scholarship.

If the scholar is competent and reacts responsibly to the dictates of prudence, there can be no limitation on academic freedom. The scholar cannot be disciplined or censored in what he or she thinks or writes in prudent statements concerning scholarship. The Catholic commitment to the intellect and reason is complete, and that commitment is fully realized within a Catholic university. Any restraint or intellectual curiosity is anathema to a Catholic university. The church requires the rich interchange of theological debate, often controversial, that only Catholic university theologians can provide.

As Bishop Donald Wuerl of Pittsburgh has said, "[I]t is usually within the world of theological discussion—sometimes heated—that a great deal of insight later recognized as fruitful development has taken and continues to take place."[32]

Because a Catholic university is committed to the view that truth is the first loyalty of the mind, the scholar within a Catholic university will be unfettered by the orthodoxy that rejects any pursuit of objective morality or values. I suggest that a Catholic university can more closely approximate the classical ideal of university education to generate, in Jefferson's phrase, not only intelligent people but virtuous people. In a word, greater symmetry between true academic freedom and university life should be found in this era of higher education in a Catholic university.

8 • Academic Freedom and the Catholic Theologian

Richard P. McBrien

This essay is not intended as an exhaustive statement on the nature of academic freedom and on the manner in which it can or ought to function in Catholic universities and colleges. I have neither the time nor the mandate to provide such a statement.[1]

I propose to sketch out in this essay what I regard as a centrist position in the debate about the academic freedom of Catholic theologians who teach in Catholic universities. I support neither the libertarian view (held by no major Catholic theologian I can think of[2]) that there are no limitations whatever on the academic freedom of Catholic theologians teaching in Catholic universities, nor the authoritarian view (held mostly by non-theologians[3]) that the academic freedom of Catholic theologians, even of those teaching in regularly accredited Catholic universities, is defined and circumscribed by the authority of the hierarchy, whether that of the Vatican or that of the local bishop.

I have structured the essay as follows: 1) the meaning and scope of academic freedom as defined by the academy; 2) the views of university presidents, theologians, canonists and bishops on the meaning and scope of academic freedom as it applies to Catholic theologians in Catholic universities; 3) The significance of the Vatican document, *Ex corde ecclesiae,* for the question of academic freedom in Catholic universities; 4) The Curran case: normative or exceptional?; and 5) Summary and Conclusion.

ACADEMIC FREEDOM: THE ACADEMY'S DEFINITION

Father Carl Peter cautions his fellow Catholic theologians against "writing or speaking about academic freedom ... rather narrowly and as if it were ... monolithic."[4] But, in the matter of the academic freedom of Catholic theologians in Catholic universities, the operative understanding *is* monolithic. Academic freedom, as applied to members of university faculties, means what the American Association of University Professors and the Association of American Colleges say it means in two major documents: *Academic Freedom and Tenure: 1940 Statement of Principles and Interpretive Comments,* and in a subsequent *Statement on Procedural Standards in Faculty Dismissal Proceedings.*[5] The 1940 Statement has been endorsed by some 140 academic associations, organizations and agencies, including the Association of American Law Schools, the American Association for Higher Education, the American Council of Learned Societies, the Council of Independent Colleges, the American Catholic Historical Association, the American Catholic Philosophical Association, the College Theology Society, the American Academy of Religion, the Association for the Sociology of Religion, the American

Society of Christian Ethics, the Association of Theological Schools, the National Education Association, and the Society of Biblical Literature.

Therefore, the AAC/AAUP definition of academic freedom and its subsequent guidelines for its protection through peer review, tenure and due process do not simply reflect one of the "faces" of academic freedom. The AAC/ AAUP understanding of academic freedom and of the procedures that are designed to protect it *is* the operative understanding that applies to all faculty in all accredited universities that have subscribed to that understanding, individually or through their appropriate academic associations. Within the American academy, that understanding has been almost universally acknowledged and accepted.

In their pastoral letter of 1980, "Catholic Higher Education and the Church's Pastoral Mission," the U.S. Catholic bishops explicitly affirmed that Catholic institutions of higher learning must abide by the same academic standards that govern other universities and colleges: "The Catholic identity of a college or university is effectively manifested only in a context of academic excellence. Policies, standards, curricula, governance and administration should accord, therefore, with the norms of quality accepted in the wider academic community."[6]

The norms "accepted in the wider academic community" include the guarantee and protection of academic freedom 1) in research and publication, 2) in teaching within the institution and 3) in extramural utterances and actions, through peer review, tenure and due process. The AAC/AAUP statements do recognize that the religious or other aims of an institution may impose a limit on academic freedom, but those limits "should be clearly stated in writing at the time of the appointment."[7]

Until the mid-sixties (the time of the Second Vatican Council), Catholic higher education paid no significant attention to the standards that governed other American universities and colleges. Catholic institutions adopted an aloof and suspicious attitude toward their secular and non-Catholic counterparts.[8] As Edward Power, author of the only history of Catholic higher education in America, pointed out: "from the outset, all [Catholic] schools from primary through college grades were preoccupied with preserving tenets of faith and with teaching policies ensuring the allegiance of Catholic people to their Church."[9] Indeed, Charles Curran has found no evidence that any Catholic educator or author before 1960 "proposed publicly that Catholic colleges and universities should accept the general American understanding of academic freedom."[10] Because of this stance, educators outside the network of Catholic institutions simply assumed the truth of George Bernard Shaw's dismissive dictum that a Catholic university is a contradiction in terms.

Relating the story of who, when, where, how and why Catholics came to accept the principle of academic freedom is beyond the scope of this paper. It is sufficient to point to the now famous Land O'Lakes Statement of 1967 as marking the decisive change. The meeting of some 26 leaders of Catholic higher education occurred under the auspices of the North American region of the International Federation of Catholic Universities. The conference was hosted by the president of the IFCU, Father Theodore M. Hesburgh, C.S.C., who was also president of the University of Notre Dame. Indeed, it was Hesburgh then and over the next 20 years who exercised the dominant leadership within the U.S. Catholic educational community and who led Catholic universities and colleges from the backwater to the mainstream of higher education in America.

The opening paragraph of the Land O'Lakes Statement speaks for itself:

> The Catholic university today must be a university in the full sense of the word, with a strong commitment to and concern for academic excellence. To perform its teaching and research functions effectively the Catholic university must have a true autonomy and academic freedom in the face of authority of whatever kind, lay

or clerical, external to the academic community itself. To say this is simply to assert that institutional autonomy and academic freedom are essential conditions of life and growth and indeed of survival for Catholic universities as for all universities.[11]

This dramatic shift within the Catholic higher education establishment would not have been possible—nor would it have been subsequently embraced by other Catholics—had it not been for the Second Vatican Council, with its emphasis on dialogue with the modern world, freedom of inquiry and of expression, the autonomy of the state, ecumenism, and so forth.[12] Nor could this new vision have been implemented effectively were it not for another revolutionary shift—namely, the transition in Catholic universities and colleges from boards of trustees dominated by clergy and religious to predominantly lay boards of trustees. This transition insured the institutional autonomy of Catholic universities an autonomy that, alongside academic freedom, is one of the twin pillars of a university's academic integrity and credibility. Typically, Hesburgh took the lead when, in 1967, he transformed the board of trustees at the University of Notre Dame from a board dominated by members of his own Congregation of Holy Cross to one dominated by laypersons.

ACADEMIC FREEDOM AND THE CATHOLIC THEOLOGIAN: DIFFERING VIEWS

There is a near unanimity of agreement among Catholic university and college presidents on the essential importance of academic freedom and institutional autonomy for their respective institutions, and on the meaning and scope of both, as outlined above. When the Vatican's Congregation for Catholic Education released the first draft of its Proposed Schema for a Pontifical Document on Catholic Universities,[13] 110 Catholic college and university presidents strongly criticized it.[14] One sentence in the synthesis of their reactions is especially applicable to the subject of this paper: "The real crux of the document is perceived by many to be the assertion of a power on the part of the bishop to control theologians (Norms, Chapter IV, Article 31) and to assure 'orthodoxy' in their teaching."[15]

The views of nearly all these presidents are reliably represented by such leading Catholic educators as Hesburgh, Father J. Donald Monan, S.J., president of Boston College, and Father Joseph O'Hare, S.J., president of Fordham University.

Hesburgh's views have been expressed so often and in such widely diverse sources that it would be impractical, not to say unnecessary, to attempt a complete listing and synthesis. His *America* article, "The Vatican and American Catholic Higher Education," offers a more than adequate statement of his position.

> The central concern about the norms [in the first draft of the Vatican schema] is that they basically run counter to the central reality and requirement of *any* university, namely, that it possess academic freedom and autonomy to do what universities do and what they do alone. . .
>
> Obviously, if church or state or any power outside the university can dictate who can teach and who can learn, the university is not free and, in fact, is not a true university where the truth is sought and taught. It is, rather, a place of political or religious indoctrination. The latter is prefectly fitting for a catechetical center, but not for a university.[16]

When asked for his reaction to the first two drafts of the proposed Vatican schema, Monan, president of Boston College, expressed the concern that

> statements of that sort really could call into question the reputation for high professional standards and integrity enjoyed by U.S. universities, and indirectly would infringe upon the autonomy and authority of university trustees, who have the ultimate responsibility for university policies and operations.

Monan acknowledged that a local bishop may feel it his duty and right to indicate to his people that a particular professor's teaching or writing is not consonant with the official teaching of the church. Indeed, Archbishop Rembert Weakland of Milwaukee did that in the case of Professor Daniel Maguire, a member of the department of theology at Marquette University, whose views on abortion have been described, rightly or wrongly, as "prochoice." "But it is an altogether different matter," Father Monan continued, "for the bishop to have a right —let alone the duty—to impede or directly reprimand a university faculty member in the conduct of his or her teaching or research functions within the university."[17]

Finally, O'Hare, president of Fordham University, has explicitly contrasted the views of Pope John Paul II and those of the Catholic college and university presidents in the United States on the central topic of this essay— namely, the academic freedom of the Catholic theologian in the Catholic university. The pope had suggested in an address before representatives of U.S. Catholic universities at Xavier University, New Orleans, on 12 September 1987, that theologians serve the church by assisting bishops in their teaching ministry. For this reason, bishops must be considered integral participants in the life of the Catholic university.[18]

By contrast, O'Hare observed that the "authors of the Land O'Lakes Statement (and, for the most part their successors in American Catholic universities today) would understand the complementary roles of bishops and theologians somewhat differently." It is true, he conceded, that the theologian must recognize the teaching authority of the bishop and carefully distinguish his or her own teaching from the official teaching of the church. "But the special charism of the theologian is not derived from the bishop's, and, in this sense, the theologian is not simply an assistant to the bishop."

O'Hare continued: "If theology is to be respected within the university, the theologian must enjoy the academic freedom granted to other scholars, even while the theologian respects the special nature of his discipline and its ecclesiastical relationship."[19]

Bishop Donald W. Wuerl of Pittsburgh, in a paper given at the Newman Center, University of Massachusetts, 5 August 1988, has insisted, over against these Catholic university presidents, that the bishops have the "final" decision on disputed matters pertaining to Catholic theology.[20] After there has been sufficient "dialogue, discussion and even disagreement," Wuerl asserts, we "cross a line from discussion about various theological conclusions to the approbation and applicaton of the conclusions."[21] But in this rendering of the case, the bishops' decision seems to be external to the academic process. Indeed, Wuerl suggests that the bishops exercise the same supervisory role over theologians that the U.S. Supreme Court exercises over the entire judicial system.[22]

The views of Catholic theologians themselves on the matter of academic freedom are generally in harmony with those of the overwhelming majority of Catholic university and college presidents. Over 750 Catholic theologians endorsed a letter of concern, drafted and sponsored by former presidents of the Catholic Theological Society of America and the College Theology Society, regarding the impending action of the Vatican's Congregation for the Doctrine of the Faith removing Curran's canonical mission to teach Catholic theology in the ecclesiastical degree program at The Catholic University of America.[23] Various statements and documents issued by the Catholic Theological Society of America, the principal professional association of Catholic theologians in the United States and Canada, have been fashioned along the lines of what I have described as a centrist position.[24]

Father Avery Dulles, S.J., one of Curran's former colleagues in the department of theology at CUA, argues a position that is practically identical with Curran's and my own; namely, that "[t]he Catholic theologian who wishes to remain a Catholic is bound to accept the definitive or irreformable doctrine of the magisterium and must be favorably disposed to accepting whatever the magisterium puts forth as obligatory doctrine."[25] Although Dulles suggests that Catholic theology and the Catholic university cannot be bound, without qualification, by the secular standard of academic freedom because the "prevalent secular theories of academic freedom are not fully satisfactory,"[26] he also insists that "[u]nless the statutes so provide, I do not see how the Holy See or the bishops could intervene directly in the working of a civilly chartered university by dismissing a professor or preventing a course from being taught."[27] In other words, the standards of the academy, not of the church, are determinative. Only in those instances where the statutes do, in fact, stipulate the right of the institution "to hire in its department of theology only professors who have received some kind of license or mission from ecclesiastical authorities" would the case be otherwise.[28] But Dulles concedes that in the United States "this type of arrangement will presumably be rare," whereas it is "not so rare in other countries."[29] For all practical purposes, this is a non-problem in the United States. It is the Curran case that has made it appear to be a major problem.

Let me repeat that, because it is the major practical assertion of this entire paper: the problem of the academic freedom of Catholic theologians teaching in Catholic universities in the United States is, for all practical purposes, a *non*-problem. The Curran case at CUA was an exception to the rule because CUA is an exception to the rule. Apart from those rare instances where the statutes of a Catholic institution require some form of ecclesiastical licensing and where the civil law approves of that condition, the problem is a *non*-problem. Had Curran been a tenured professor at the University of Notre Dame or at Duquesne University at the time of his censure by the Vatican, his academic status within the department of theology at either institution would not, could not, have been affected.

The views of Catholic canon lawyers are also generally consistent with those of the presidents and the theologians. Father Ladislas Orsy, S.J., of the faculty of canon law at The Catholic University of America, notes that

> [T]here are good reasons to argue that in the United States there is an ancient custom of academic freedom and institutional autonomy observed by Catholic universities as well as by others. If the existence of such custom is eventually proved to the satisfaction of the local Ordinary, he may tolerate its continued observance notwithstanding the fact that the old custom is in conflict with the new law.[30]

Father James Provost, a colleague of Orsy's at CUA and a leading figure in the Canon Law Society of America over the years, has taken a similar position, arguing against the application of the canonical mission (or mandate) to Catholic theologians teaching in Catholic universities, as required by canon 812. The "net effect," Provost argues, would be "to eliminate what United States colleges and universities mean by legitimate autonomy and self-regulation."[31]

The only significant divergence from the practical consensus among presidents, theologians and canonists occurs at the episcopal level. Very few bishops have addressed the question of academic freedom according to the terms stated in this collection of essays. Of those who have addressed the question, the prevailing viewpoint (which I have referred to as an "emerging party line"[32]) rejects the application of traditional American standards of academic freedom to the Catholic theologian teaching in Catholic universities and colleges. The "emerging party line," espoused by Bishop Wuerl himself, Archbishop Daniel Pilarczyk of Cincinnati, and Archbishop Oscar Lipscomb of Mobile, contains some of the following elements:

1. There are two models of academic freedom: one secular and the other Catholic. The former is

"unlimited" and "unfettered" (Wuerl); the latter is limited.

2. The academic freedom of the Catholic theologian is limited by revelation and the teaching authority of the church.

3. The teaching authority of the Church is not "external" to the process of theological development. It is "internal" to it (Lipscomb).

4. Bishops make the "final" decision on what is true and what is false, what is right and what is wrong (Wuerl). Indeed, the bishops' intervention functions as "peer judgment" does in the sciences (Lipscomb).

5. Theologians engage in "speculation," and a Catholic university is "a kind of speculative think tank" (Pilarczyk). However, the outcome of such speculation is never to touch the realm of moral or pastoral practice.[33]

These bishops' views are generally reflected in the recently published Vatican document on Catholic universities, *Ex corde ecclesiae*, to which I shall now turn my attention.

THE VATICAN DOCUMENT ON CATHOLIC UNIVERSITIES

Pope John Paul II's Apostolic Constitution on Catholic Universities, *Ex corde ecclesiae*,[34] speaks positively and supportively about the mission of a Catholic university and even about its need for institutional autonomy and academic freedom (para. 12), although, somewhat ominously, the document adds a condition to the affirmation of academic freedom and intitutional autonomy; namely, "so long as the rights of the individual person and of the community are preserved within the confines of the truth and the common good." It is not at all clear what this qualification means.

The Apostolic Constitution also acknowledges that the "future of Catholic Universities depends to a great extent on the competent and dedicated service of lay Catholics" (para. 25), and encourages dialogue and collaboration across religious, cultural and scientific lines.

The General Norms make a clear distinction between two kinds of Catholic universities: the one established by the church and operating under some kind of ecclesiastical sponsorship, and the other established by Catholics (religious or lay) independently of official ecclesiastical authority (art. 1, n. 3). The distinction is important because the Apostolic Constitution recognizes that, while universities of the first type must have their statutes and governing documents approved by "competent ecclesiastical Authority," universities of the second type do not. Ideally, these universities should try to conform to the General Norms, but the document recognizes that their statues and the civil law of the place have to be observed.

The positive tone of the Apostolic Constitution, the brevity and general character of its practical norms, and its acknowledgement of important differences among Catholic universities have pleased most of the document's potential critics. But this is not to say that the text is without problems.

There are at least two undetonated bombs that, under the right (or is it "wrong"?) conditions, could explode at some time in the future. Individuals and institutions could still get hurt. The first problem has to do with the scope of academic freedom, and the second has to do with the role of the local bishop in the internal affairs of the university.

The document seems to suggest that not all faculty members enjoy full academic freedom. Specifically, Catholic theologians in Catholic universities enjoy academic freedom only "so long as they are faithful to [the] principles and methods" of their discipline (para. 29). That means, according to this document, respecting the authority of the bishops and assenting to Catholic doctrine "according to the degree of authority with which it is taught" (para. 29).

Elsewhere, the document carves out a remarkably large

place for the activity of the local bishop in the life of
the Catholic university (para. 28 and art. 5, n. 2). He has
"the right and duty to watch over the preservation and
strengthening of their Catholic character," and of taking
"initiatives necessary to resolve" problems related there-
to. Furthermore, he is to be kept informed about the
university and its activities (art. 5, n. 2).

To be sure, these two items—the theologian's academic freedom and the role of the local bishop—are subject to a benign interpretation. But they are also open
to a less benign one. And therein lie two potential
problems.

First, the document seeks to limit the academic freedom of Catholic theologians indirectly rather than directly. It does so by affirming that, while theologians
should enjoy full academic freedom within Catholic
universities alongside other scholars and teachers, such
freedom is conditioned by the theologian's fidelity to the
"principles and methods" of the discipline.

"Since theology seeks an understanding of revealed
truth whose authentic interpretation is entrusted to the
Bishops of the Church," the Apostolic Constitution de-
clares, "it is intrinsic to the principles and methods of
their research and teaching in their academic discipline
that theologians respect the authority of the Bishops, and
assent to Catholic doctrine according to the degree of
authority with which it is taught" (para. 29).

An earlier Vatican document on the ecclesial vocation
of Catholic theologians made no allowance whatever for
public disagreement with any official teaching of the
Church, in whole or in part.[35] Thus, if that earlier document were to be normative for interpreting the Apostolic Constitution on Catholic Universities, Catholic theologians would forfeit the protection of academic freedom
in Catholic universities whenever they expressed public
disagreement with any official church teaching.

On the other hand, the Apostolic Constitution calls
only for "respect" for the authority of the bishops and

recognizes that official teachings have different degrees of authority. This latter point was a bone of contention in the dispute between the Vatican Congregation for the Doctrine of the Faith and Charles Curran of The Catholic University of America. Perhaps, therefore, the language of this document is sufficiently nuanced (or ambiguous) to allow for a benign interpretation.

A second potential problem with the new Apostolic Constitution is the active role it accords a local bishop in the internal life of a Catholic university. According to the Constitution, even when local bishops do not enter into the internal governance of the university, they "should be seen not as external agents but as participants in the life of the Catholic university." The language is that of Pope John Paul II, employed originally in his talk at Xavier University in New Orleans in 1987. What does that language mean, precisely? It is not clear from the text of the Apostolic Constitution.

Later, in the General Norms section of the document, it is asserted that the local bishop has "the right and the duty to watch over the preservation and strengthening of their Catholic character."

"If problems should arise concerning this Catholic character," the Apostolic Constitution continues, "the local Bishop is to take the initiatives necessary to resolve the matter, working with the competent university authorities in accordance with established procedures. . ." (art. 5, n. 2). A footnote indicates that such procedures in the case of independent Catholic universities are "to be determined by Episcopal Conferences or other Assemblies of Catholic Hierarchy" (n. 52).

But, of course, no ecclesiastical body, including an episcopal conference, can establish procedures which are in violation of the statutes of the university in question or of civil law. Another loophole closed? A second potential problem removed? No one can really say at this early stage. Somewhere down the road these two items could prove genuinely troublesome in dioceses with a doctrinally rigid and pastorally authoritarian bishop, on the one hand, and a weak university administration, on the other.

THE CURRAN CASE: NORMATIVE OR EXCEPTIONAL?

Given the unpleasant possibility with which I ended the preceding section, one might legitimately ask if the Curran case was a harbinger of things to come. In other words, is the Curran case normative for the future, or is it rather an exceptional one (as I have suggested above)?

In my judgment, the Curran case may have distorted the controversy over the academic freedom of Catholic theologians in Catholic universities because it *is* an exceptional rather than a normative case. Only at The Catholic University of America could a U.S. court have ruled, *on the basis of contract law*, against an appeal similar to Charles Curran's.[36]

The Catholic University has a "unique and special relationship with the Holy See," Judge Frederick H. Weisberg of the Superior Court of the District of Columbia wrote in his decision of 28 February 1989. Therefore, "the conflict between the university's commitment to academic freedom and its unwavering fealty to the Holy See is direct and unavoidable."

"On such issues," he continued, "the university may choose for itself on which side of that conflict it wants to come down, and nothing in its contract with Professors Curran or any other faculty member promises that it will always come down on the side of academic freedom."[37]

Apart from the special circumstances at CUA, we have had no case where a Catholic theologian teaching in a Catholic university has had tenure revoked, or even under threat of revocation, because of an ecclesiastical intervention in violation of the almost universally recognized American standards of academic freedom and institutional autonomy. In 11 years as chairman of the Department of Theology at the University of Notre Dame, I encountered or experienced no such case, in actuality or at the level of threat. In the final accounting, therefore, the problem of academic freedom for Catholic theologians teaching in Catholic universities is a non-problem—at the *institutional* level.

If, however, Catholic universities were voluntarily to allow for a CUA-type relationship with the Vatican or with the local hierarchy where, by a change of their statutes, their Catholic theologians would become vulnerable to the same kind of action that was taken against Curran, and with the same kind of outcome, then Catholic universities would face two consequences: 1) they would have to remove theology from the academic life of the university and confine it to the department of campus ministry or some other nonaccredited sector of the university; and/or 2) they would run the risk, at worst, of losing their academic accreditation or, at best, their good reputation among peer institutions.

Unless and until Catholic universities willingly enter into a new relationship with the Vatican, with the national episcopal conference, or with individual diocesan bishops, the only level at which the Catholic theologian teaching in a Catholic university is still vulnerable is the *ecclesiastical*. A theologian's diocesan bishop or religious superior might, on his own initiative or by order of the Vatican, attempt to recall the theologian to his or her diocese of incardination or religious community for reassignment. In such an instance, the theologian's *academic* position would not be in jeopardy, but his or her *ministerial* and/or *religious* status would. But that is another question entirely, and it is beyond the direct concern or scope of this paper.

SUMMARY AND CONCLUSION

What I have attempted to do in this paper was to sketch out a centrist position on the highly controverted question of the academic freedom of Catholic theologians teaching in Catholic universities.

It is a centrist position because it acknowledges, over against a libertarian view, that there *are* limits beyond which a Catholic theologian cannot go without forfeiting his or her right to be regarded as a *Catholic* theologian. Those limits are imposed by revelation in general and by the official teachings of the church in particular.

It is a centrist position, secondly, because it insists, over against an authoritarian view, that Catholic theologians enjoy the same academic freedom that any other member of a Catholic university faculty enjoys. In other words, even if a Catholic theologian were declared by the Vatican, or by a national episcopal conference, or by a diocesan bishop, to be no longer suitable or eligible to teach Catholic theology (the terms of the judgment against Curran), that declaration would have no effect on the theologian's status *as a faculty member*, even within a department that grants ecclesiastical degrees and/or that has among its student body candidates for presbyteral ordination. Only the theologian's academic peers, i.e., fellow theologians, acting in accordance with the statutes and faculty handbook of the university, could generate that result. An ecclesiastical declaration regarding a theologian's Catholicity can have only ecclesiastical consequences.

Whether this qualification would satisfy those who hold what I have called a libertarian position, I don't know. Whether it would satisfy the concerns (and fears) of those who hold what I have called an authoritarian position, I would doubt.

This centrist position respects, on the one hand, the canons of academic freedom and institutional autonomy that are almost universally recognized and enforced in universities and colleges in the United Sates, and, on the other hand, respects the right and even the duty of the official church to render public judgment on the orthodoxy and Catholicity of its theologians.

9 • Truth, Cultural Pluralism and Academic Freedom

George S. Worgul, Jr.

Freedom in the academy exists to pursue and serve truth. The faculty and students of every discipline have, not only the right, but also the duty to embrace this noble enterprise with dedication and vigor. Likewise, the results of this search must be communicated to the larger public. This essay will argue that recent attentiveness to cultural pluralism and meaning systems challenges and requires a reappraisal of the relationship between truth and freedom.

Two brief texts will set the stage for this inquiry. In the first text, Frederich Nietzche calls into question the very reality of truth. In the second text, David Tracy notes the hermeneutical necessity of critically attending to truth claims in the process of unraveling the meaning of religious traditions.

With suspicious sages, Nietzche asked:

What, then, is truth? A mobile army of metaphors, meto-
nyms, and anthropomorphisms—in short, a sum of human
relations, which have been enhanced, transposed, and em-
bellished poetically and rhetorically, and which after long
use seem firm, canonical, and obligatory to a people: truths
are illusions about which one has forgotten that this is
what they are: metaphors which are worn out and without
sensuous power. . .[1]

If Nietzsche is correct, should we not halt our quest for
these hollow illusions? Tracy says no.

All interpreters of religion, whether believers or non-
believers, can employ something like the theologian's sixth
sense that to interpret religion at all demands being willing to put at risk one's present self-understanding in order
to converse with the claim to attention of the religious
classic. That instinctive sense is not only theologically
but also hermeneutically sound. Like the classics of art
and morality, the religious classics demand that we pay
attention to their claims to truth if we are to understand
their meaning at all.[2]

These two texts bring us to the central issue: what
is the relationship between pluralism and truth? Is there
a way to understand the legitimacy of pluralism (ambiguity) and still affirm a unicity for truth within its multi-
plicity? Nietzsche correctly warns us against a rarified
view of truth that is disconnected from concrete life.
Tracy correctly warns us against any attempt to excise
the question of truth from an investigation of classics.
Perhaps the best starting point toward a relatively adequate answer to our question is to attempt to clarify what
we mean by truth.

Classical Thomistic epistomology distinguished ontological truth from logical truth. Ontological truth was
viewed as a property or characteristic of reality itself:
ens et verum convertuntur. Being qua being is knowable
and intelligible. Truth is a transcendental relationship
between being and the human faculty of knowledge. It
is the ontological truth of being that is the possibility

of logical truth. When knowing corresponds to being, it is logically true. In human terms, insofar as thought in the act of judging expresses reality as it is, it expresses truth (metaphysical truth) and is itself true (logical truth).

In this view, thinking existence discovers itself from the very beginning in the open field of being. Being offers infinite possibilities to thinking and knowing. Being and knowing exist symbiotically. Thinking existence's searching movement toward truth is a response to the invitation of being to be known.

In a style quite different from that of the Thomists, nineteenth century thinkers like Coleridge, Schelling and Geothe nonetheless affirmed the Thomistic insight. Coleridge said that truth is reality itself, ultimate reality.[3] Reality is, from the start, present in and to the thinking subject. This is the source and condition of possibility of all consciousness and thought. Schelling argued that truth possesses us before we posses truth.[4] The presence of Being as a whole in and to the mind constitutes the mind itself and makes thought possible.

Human thought, then, is the process of converting universal truth/being, present and active in the mind, into a possession of the individual mind by means of expression. However, the human mind will never possess being/universal truth actually or adequately. Coleridge called the presence of reality working in the subject, *reason*. He called the presence of reality present to the mind, *Idea*. The attempt to get at truth through forming concepts and immediate judgments he called *understanding*.[5] It is important to recognize the polarity between reason and understanding. Reason is at work in understanding, and the exercise of understanding is continually operative in the presence of reason. Without reason, understanding can produce only hollow constructs without content. With reason, understanding can attain truth intuitively comprehended and contemplated through the mediating process of conceptual reasoning. Yet, a distance always remains between thought and truth insofar as thought is necessarily conceptual.

Concepts are not truth but tools of human construction. Truth is, however, mediated through these concepts. Concepts open limited windows of opportunity that allow us to know truth.

Geothe expands the view of Coleridge and Schelling by demonstrating that the truth communicates itself not only through spoken language but also through nature, life and art.[6] Inspired by J. Hamann, the first great opponent of the Enlightenment's conceptual rationalism, Goethe understood visible nature itself as a language. Truth, for Goethe, is the whole, the comprehensive. This whole always remains transcendent. As such it is *unzuganglich* (inaccessible) and *unaussprechlich* (unspeakable). Therefore, Goethe advises that we not speak about it too much. Nevertheless, truth does "appear." Truth indirectly betrays its active presence in nature, in poetry, in art and in human life. Life, art and nature are ways to truth. Truth is their highest aim.

Goethe dismissed any idea that truth can be attained as a definitive possession at the endpoint of discursive reasoning. With nature, art and poetry, discursive reasoning may function as a medium for truth. However, truth is grasped intuitively in the contemplation of its symbolic mediums. Goethe also notes that the mediation of truth is conditioned in two ways. First, there must be a counterpoint or antipole, something which is contrary to the idea and which conditions the possibility of the idea's going out of itself. Second, the appearance of truth in its medium is conditioned by the social and personal factors that affect our human way of seeing things and representing them. No one spontaneously attains pure phenomena or primordial sense experience. Goethe claims that science and art have the noble role of purifying our way of representing experience so that we may see in our representations and ordinary perceptions the *Urphenomenon*. This will allow us to approach closer to truth. Yet Geothe rightly notes that our human contemplation of truth in works of art, poetry and science is always mixed with error. Human creative activity simultaneously unveils and veils truth.

Surely our question, *What is Truth?*, is not a question about the exact knowledge of facts. Facts are important as mediums of truth. But our question is a question about meaning. What is the reality in which we gradually awake to consciousness? What is its meaning? What is the meaning of our existence in it? What is our part in the endless ·unfolding process of nature and history into which we have been thrown for a short cosmic moment?

The question of truth reveals that human beings are incurable philosophers. Human beings continually ask why until an answer is discovered to explain our life's adventure. Like actors pushed on stage without knowing the pieces and the parts, we struggle to create, learn and master our roles.

The question of meaning is inseparable connected with the question of reality. *Something real has meaning, acquires meaning, receives meaning, gives meaning.* What? and What for? are essentially conjoined. The answer to the question What for? is the ultimate answer to the question What? Being is by nature a being for or toward, and that toward which or for which it exists is its highest goal and most true description.

The question of meaning is ultimately one question: the meaning of the whole. If the whole is not meaningful, neither are any of its partial expressions. Moreover, just as truth possesses us before we can appropriate it or come to possesses it in that inadequate way that is possible for us, and this being possessed by truth is the possibility of all thought, knowledge and consciousness, so it is with meaning. Meaning must be given to us in the root of our being before we can achieve it or create it in our concrete limited situation. In real sense, truth is meaning. On this issue Heidegger must be consulted.

When Heidegger speaks of *Das Wesen der Wahrheit,*[7] the essence of truth, he means the ground of the inner possibility of something that previously and generally is admitted as known. Truth consists in the agreement or assimilation by way of representation . The representation (*vorstellung*) and represented (*vorgestellte*) possess this sameness or agreement. *Vorstellen* is not a psychological condition but simply my allowing an object to stand over against me (*Gegenstand*). This condition requires openness both in the object and in the subject. This openness is not created by the subject but is the field in which the subject exists. The human person finds itself in the open and holds to something (Seiende, the being) that opens itself to the subject. This being can be represented in language or speech only because the representing subject is guided by something that points the subject to say the being as it is. The subject must be taken over by a previously given rule of all true representation. What however, asks Heidegger, is the ground of this inner direction of the subject? His answer is freedom. Heidegger includes the common sense notion of freedom as a choice of alternatives in his understanding of freedom. Moreover, he grounds this level of freedom in a reality much more fundamental. He writes:

> Before all this, freedom is a being admitted in the un-concealing of being as such (*eingelassenheit*). The un-concealdness itself is preserved in the existent letting oneself into (*Sicheinlassen*) by which the openness of the open i.e., the Da is constituted.[8]

This critical sentence requires comment.

Freedom is described as letting the being be what it is. This is not simply indifference or mere passivity. It is an active passivity, a commitment or risking oneself into the being. This is not so much a conscious choice but the situation that constitutes human existence as a human. To "let be" is to expose oneself in the un-concealedness of being. It is only in this risk of human existence that the openness of the open is constituted. Without Dasein, it would make no sense to speak of the openness of being. It is ek-sistense as exposedness to being that gives rise to history. Freedom, then, is in the first place something that possesses the human person. Freedom, in Heidegger's view, frees the human from nature and places the human in the realm of free choice and ethical commitment. Freedom constitutes the individual endowed with choice and standing under the rule of what must be realized. Freedom is a vocation not only to know being also to realize or attain its fullness.

Heidegger insists that the unveiling of being is necessarily its veiling. Dasein is simultaneously and necessarily existing and in-sisting. By letting be a particular being as an act of unveiling, the human conceals being as a whole. However, it can be no other way since there is no human act or unveiling the whole of being. Consequently, the whole of being in which we exist by insisting is a mystery that cannot be recovered in conscious thought.

There is in truth both a *Wesen* and an *Unwesen*. Just as the Wesen of truth grounds the possibility of right sayings, so the Unwesen is the ground of inescapable error. Both the Wesen and the Unwesen are one. Error is not simply the result of an accident or fault on our part. Dasein exists in truth through existing, and Dasein exists in error through insisting. The more one actually knows about particular beings, the more the sight and consciousness of being as a whole is obscured and its mystery obscured. The accumulation of particular knowledge tends to obscure truth. This eventually leads to *Seinvergessenheit*, the oblivion of being. Heidegger judges this to be the situation of Western civilization, which has become exclusively concerned with exact science and practical aims achieved by calculated thinking. This must be overcome by meditative thinking that recovers and respects the mystery of being itself.

Since human efforts at disclosing truth both unveil and veil, pluralism in any science (especially those whose stated purpose is to reflect of the meaning of the whole of reality) should not only be expected but deemed necessary. No single viewpoint or system can ever exhaust the truth of reality. Each partial insight, no matter how adequate to its specific purpose, ultimately remains partial and requires correction. Moreover, human insights are always human interpretations. There is simply no alternative to knowing than to know in the prejudiced condition of concrete cultural life.

While philosophical thinkers have alluded to the situationalism of meaning, the challenge of inculturation undertaken by cultural/theological anthropologists has highlighted the role and function of meaning systems. In a real sense, the challenge of inculturation grounds the issue of pluralism and the problem of truth in living experience.

A text from Naylors's *Daybreak In The Dark Continent* published in 1908 boldly sets the context.

> Christianity, the truest civilization, works in Africa as everywhere. through transformed character and not by external force. This civilization introduced by the missionary gradually radiates until dominates the whole community.[9]

This endemic view, which dominated nineteenth and early twentieth century missionary activities, judged all non-Western cultures to be inferior, hypostatized Western civilization Christianity and identified truth with Western civilization's meaning system.

Fortunately, the period between 1920 and 1960 the gradual erosion and collapse of this ideological imperialism. It was replaced by vision or theme of adaptation or accommodation, a theme that dominated the 1959 International Study Week on Liturgy and the Missions and formal acceptance by Catholicism at the Second Vatican Council. At the International Study Week, Cardinal Gracias remarked:

> If the church is an objective social reality, She is not bound to conform herself to cultural divisions. She can take whatever forms and institutions she needs from any culture and organize them into a new unity which is the external expression of her spirit and the organ of her mission in the world.[10]

Bishop Van Cauwalaert noted:

> Adaptation consists in establishing a bridge between the natural virtue of religion as it is practiced by the Africans and the Catholic cult as it springs from revelation and the traditional practice of the Church. She must establish harmony between those two terms, not by the way of equating but by way of "assumption"; namely it is the Christian cult which must assume to itself the authentically religious values of the American Civilization.[11]

Bishop Blomjous stressed:

> This is the period in which adaptation is especially important, but an adaptation in the right sense. Not an adaptation of Christianity to non-Western cultures, Christianity as such is above or outside the different human cultures—but an adaptation in the sense of being ready to understand an appreciate non-Western cultures, and of being open enough to take these other cultural values into Christianity and through Christianity into our Western cultural heritage.[12]

The vision of adaptation represented in these speeches and "canonized" at the Second Vatican Council was surely an advance. However, it too is limited. While an attempt is made to differentiate Christianity from its particular cultural incarnation, and values inherent in non-Western cultures are recognized as true and legitimate, the correlation was understood to be juxtapositional rather than critical. Adaptation was an issue of language and custom. Little attention was paid to the intrinsic worth, value, meaning and truth of non-Western, non-Christian culture/religion in its own right. Christianity was still viewed as a meaning system with truth that approached a culture from without, albeit always ready to adapt to the culture so that it might nonetheless transform it. Western Christianity still controls and judges what is an appropriate and acceptable adaptation. The shift in understanding from adaptation to inculturation during the seventies and into our own day sought to alleviate these limitations.

During the last two decades, three terms; inculturation, indigenization and contextualization, have been employed almost interchangeably to address the appropriate interchange between Christianity and non-Western
cultures. In 1981 Peter Sarpong wrote:

> Inculturation means indigenization. I understand by in-
> digenization the process through which something origi-
> nating from outside a culture is made to take root in that
> culture and become native to it. Christianity becomes
> indigenous to us the Christian message and its institu-
> tional form enter our cultural unit and undergo definition,
> explanation, adoption, reinterpretation and new discovery
> so that the people of my cultural unit can recognize that
> it belongs to them.[13]

What exactly distinguishes inculturation from adaptation or accommodation? In my judgment, the key difference is a transformation of the fundamental horizon
within which the relationship of Christianity and non-
Christian culture is understood. The perspective of
inculturation allows the indigenous culture to be itself.
If this culture is transformed by Christianity, it is
transformed from within and its concrete forms are
generated from within. Kenneth Pike's differentiation of
etic and emic viewpoints is important here. He notes;

> The etic viewpoint studies behavior as from outside of
> a particular system, and as an essential initial approach
> to an alien system. The emic viewpoint results from
> studying behavior as from inside the system.
>   An etic system may be set up by criteria or logical plan
> whose relevance is external to the system being studied.
> The discovery or setting up of the emic system requires
> the inclusion of criteria relevant to the internal function-
> ing of the system itself. Emic criteria require a knowledge
> of the total system to which they are relative and from
> which they ultimately draw their significance.[14]

Clearly, the horizon of adaptation reflects an etic viewpoint, whereas inculturation, indigenization and contextualization reflect an emic viewpoint. What, however,

is the relationship of these horizons to the issue of theological pluralism and the problem of truth?

First, inculturation with its emic horizon recognizes theological pluralism as a necessity. Theological pluralism is grounded, not as a preference or sign of intellectual openness, but as the product of legitimate cultural diversity expressed in plural meaning systems. Theological pluralism emerges from a plurality of living experiences which are always, if they are real, culturally mediated.

Second, any attempt to judge the relative adequacy of truth claims attached to these meaning systems and the theological articulation emerging from them should first be undertaken from within. Without adequate experience and understanding, a true judgment simply cannot be undertaken.

Third, the evaluation of these meaning systems in relationship to alternative meaning system and their theological elaboration should not be subject to historical canonization or to an authoritative whim rooted in subjective familiarity or preference. The temptation to cultural imperialism, reflected in an etic viewpoint, must be avoided.

Fourth, while the perspective of this essay claims that truth is unavoidable mediated by meaning systems that give rise to pluralism, it does not therefore ascribe to a relativistic vision of truth or deny its unicity. On the contrary, truth possesses a unicity. Truth can be grasped— or, better, we can be grasped by truth—but only in its real/fragmented mediation. This is not relativism, but a recognition of the human condition. Authentic pluralism, as a expression of the rich possibilities of life experiences rather than being a distraction from truth, may in fact lead us to its reality. Theological pluralism, in effect, is our ally in coming to a deeper understanding of truth's mystery.

In a sense we have arrived at a place similar to that occupied by Heidegger. Just as truth forces philosophy beyond metaphysics, so truth forces theology beyond itself to a living active meditative faith.

If the members of the academy are to fulfill their responsibility to search for truth, they must become keenly attentive to the reality and value of pluralism and the dynamics of inculturation. In turn, attentiveness to inculturation and plural meaning systems will enhance their freedom (in a Heideggarian sense of openness) and allow their glimpses of relative truth to reflect more clearly and completely the evasive unicity and wholeness of truth itself.

Notes

Notes to Essay 1/Hanigan

1. Richard A. McCormick, S.J., "L'Affaire Curran," *America* 154 (5 April 1986). The discussion can readily be followed in the pages of this journal. See, for example, Gerald P. Fogarty, "Dissent at Catholic University: The Case of Henry Poels," *America* 156 (11 October 1986); Richard P. McBrien, "Academic Freedom in Catholic Universities: The Emergence of a Party Line," *America* 159 (3 December 1988); Avery Dulles, "The Teaching Mission of the Church and Academic Freedom," *America* 162 (21 April 1990); Timothy S. Healy, "Probity and Freedom on the Border: Learning and Belief in the Catholic University," *America* 163 (30 June–7 July 1990); Richard A. McCormick, S.J., and Richard P. McBrien, "L'Affaire Curran II," *America* 163 (8–15 September 1990).

2. William W. May (ed.), *Vatican Authority and American Catholic Dissent: The Curran Case and Its Consequences* (New York: Crossroads, 1988); see esp. the essays by Richard A. McCormick, S.J., Joseph Komonchak, Anne E. Patrick, Joseph A. O'Hare and Rodger Van Allen. Charles E. Curran and Richard A. McCormick, S.J. (eds.), *Readings in Moral Theology No. 6: Dissent in the Church* (New York/Mahwah: Paulist Press, 1989); see the essays by Mark D. Jordan, Bernard Haring, Kevin Kelly and Christine Gudorf. Curran's own views are most comprehensively available in Charles E. Curran, *Faithful Dissent* (Kansas City, MO: Sheed and Ward, 1986).

3. Canon 812 in the New Code of Canon Law reads: "It is necessary that those who teach theological disciplines in any institute of higher studies have a mandate from the competent ecclesiastical authority." James A. Corriden, Thomas J. Green, Donald E. Heintschel (eds.), *The Code of Canon Law: A Text and Commentary* (New York/Mahwah: Paulist Press, 1985), 575–76 for the text and comments on its meaning and application.

4. *Origins* 15/43 (10 April 1986), 706–11. See also the "Summary of Responses to Draft Schema on Catholic Universities," *Origins* 17/41 (24 March 1988), 693–705, and "A Draft Document on Catholic Higher Education," *Origins* 18, 28 (22 December 1988), 445–64.

5. *Origins* 18/40 (16 March 1989), 661, 663. See also the *Report of the Catholic Theological Society of America Committee on the Profession of Faith and the Oath of Fidelity* (Catholic Theological Society of America, 1990).

6. *Origins* 20/8 (5 July 1990), 117–26; see also Archbishop John Quinn, "Observations on Doctrinal Congregation's Instruction," *Origins* 20/13 (6 September 1990), 201–05.

7. Second Vatican Council, *Dignitatis humanae* 1 (Declaration on Religious Freedom) in Joseph Gremillion, *The Gospel of Peace and Justice: Catholic Social Teaching Since Pope John* (Maryknoll, NY: Orbis Books, 1976), 338.

8. "The Ecclesial Vocation of the Theologian," 32, sees the "ideology of philosophical liberalism, which permeates the thinking of our age," as one of the factors contributing to confusion about freedom and rights (*Origins* 20/8, p. 123).

9. Germain Grisez, "How to Deal with Theological Dissent," *Readings in Moral Theology No. 6*, 456, uses the metaphor of "a cancer growing in the Church's organs, and interfering with her vital functions."

10. In *Vatican Authority and American Catholic Dissent*, see the essays by James Hitchcock, William E. May, and to a lesser extent Michael Novak. In *Readings in Moral Theology No. 6*, see the essays by Grisez, Edward J. Berbusse, and David Fitch, S.J.

11. David Hollenbach, S.J., *Claims in Conflict: Retrieving and Renewing the Catholic Human Rights Tradition* (New York/Ramsey/Toronto: Paulist Press, 1979), and *Justice, Peace and Human Rights: American Catholic Social Ethics in a Pluralistic World* (New York: Crossroad, 1988), 87–123.

12. *Dignitatis humanae* 2; in Gremillion, 339.

13. Michael Novak, *Freedom with Justice: Catholic Social Thought and Liberal Institutions*, 2nd ed. (New Brunswick and

is never to coerce another, but to admonish and instruct, but, of course, words and behavior designed to admonish and instruct may be experienced by the recipient of them as coercive. In practice, Christian neighbor-love eschews violence in the pursuit of religious and spiritual ends. Whether the use of violence is ever morally permissible to such love for social and interpersonal purposes is another question.

30. There are, of course, some common agreements among college and university communities, but they are largely about forms and processes, not about substantive notions of what is true and good. There may be more substantive agreement on truth and values than appears on the surface, as Stout, *The Ethics of Babel*, has argued with some merit throughout his book. But the 12 year-old judgment of Robert Morrill, *Teaching Values in College* (San Francisco: Jossey-Bass Publishers, 1980), 2–3, still seems accurate. He wrote: "the autonomy and professionalization of the disciplines, the increasing hegemony and prestige of value-free scientific methodology as a model for all inquiry, and the secularization and pluralism of both our society and the university have established a new educational context. This is a strange and foreign world for moral education. In the academic community, there is little confidence about what can be known in the moral realm, and even less about why, how, and to whom it should be taught."

31. The transcendent ground is simply expressed in the assertion that we must obey God, not human beings, whenever human authority conflicts with the Divine Will.

32. "Religious freedom . . . has to do with immunity from coercion in civil society. Therefore, it leaves untouched traditional Catholic doctrine on the moral duty of men and societies toward the true religion and toward the one Church of Christ." *Dignitatis humanae* 1, in Gremillion, 338. On the meaning and importance of the formation of conscience if conscience is to be authentic, see Hanigan, 128–42.

33. *Lumen gentium* 25, in Austin Flannery, O.P. (ed.), *Vatican Council II: The Conciliar and Post Conciliar Documents* (Collegeville, MN: The Liturgical Press, 1975), 379–81. See also Ladislas Orsy, S.J., *The Church: Learning and Teaching* (Wilmington, DL: Michael Glazier, Inc., 1987), 13–78.

34. This is precisely why private disagreement is not a particularly acute problem, but public dissent is, as even "The Instruction on the Ecclesial Vocation of the Theologian" 28–32, acknowledges (*Origins* 20/8, 123).

35. Dulles, "The Teaching Mission of the Church and Academic Freedom," 399.

36. Karl Rahner, "Theologie und Lehramt," *Stimmen der*

Zeit (1980), 369, as cited by Msgr. Thomas Herron, "Reflections on the Theologian's Ecclesial Vocation," *Origins* 20/38 (28 February 1991), 627, wrote: "In principle the magisterium is not guilty of any arrogance when it censures us. Nor is a censure of this kind, a priori and fundamentally, a threat to the freedom of our theological research."

37. I have borrowed the notion of "social space" from Hannah Arendt, *On Revolution* (New York: Viking Press, 1965), 120–21; ". . . public freedom was not an inner realm into which men might escape at will from the pressures of the world, nor was it the *liberum arbitrium* which makes the will choose between alternatives. Freedom for them could exist only in public; it was a tangible, wordly reality, something created by men to be enjoyed by men rather than a gift or a capacity; it was the manmade public space—a market place which antiquity had known as the arena where freedom appears and becomes visible to all." I have discussed the notion of space and its relationship to human freedom in Hanigan, 57–62.

38. Louis Hartz, *The Liberal Tradition in America* (New York: Harcourt, Brace & World, Inc., 1955).

39. As mentioned above in the text, the mechanisms in place in American colleges and universities do little to protect faculty from various forms of economic and social peer pressure and manipulation. Let it also be said that such mechanisms are not designed to do so and that other mechanisms have a place in the university setting. The unionization of faculties to ensure adequate wages and working conditions, or the creation of alternate professional organizations are two such mechanisms.

40. *Dignitatis humanae* 13; "Among the things which concern the good of the Church and indeed the welfare of society here on earth . . . this certainly is preeminent, namely, that the Church should enjoy that full measure of freedom which her care for the salvation of men requires. . . The freedom of the Church is the fundamental principle in what concerns the relations between the Church and governments and the whole civil order." in Gremillion, 346–47. The similarity between the struggle over academic freedom and religious freedom seems to me to be very great. See John Courtney Murray, S.J., "The Problem of Religious Freedom," *Theological Studies* 25 (1964), 503–75.

41. *Lumen gentium* 21, in Flannery, 373–74, speaks of a special outpouring of the Holy Spirit through episcopal consecration so that bishops in a visible manner take the place

of Christ. Given that view of episcopal authority, one would hardly approach it with suspicion as one's first and primary attitude. The "Instruction on the Ecclesial Vocation of the Theologian," 24, *Origins* 20/8, 122–23, rightly insists on this point.

42. *Gaudium et spes* 59, in Gremillion, 295; "Instruction on the Ecclesial Vocation of the Theologian," 11 *Origins* 20/8, 120 and note 7, p. 126; also Canon 809.

43. *Code of Canon Law*, 571–76; in the commentary on Canons 807–814, the author indicates the Church's acceptance of the situation prevailing in various countries in regard to institutional autonomy and academic freedom. Its only institutional concern seems to be with ensuring its own position vis-a-vis these arrangements.

44. John Paul II, *Ex Corde Ecclesiae* ("Apostolic Constitution on Catholic Universities"), *Origins* 20/17 (4 October 1990).

45. See note 6.

46. The three references to creativity in *Ex Corde Ecclesiae* are to be found in para. 1, (*Origins* 20/17, p. 265); para. 8, (p. 268); para. 25, (p. 270).

47. To describe these references as rhetorical is not to denigrate them or dismiss them, but to recognize their function in the document. They are to found in *Ex Corde Ecclesiae*, para. 1 (*Origins* 20/17, p. 265); para. 4 (p. 267); para. 7 (p. 268); para. 21 (p. 270).

48. *Ex Corde Ecclesiae*, para. 11 (*Origins* 20/17, p. 268); para. 37 (p. 272).

49. Freedom of conscience is mentioned in *Ex Corde Ecclesiae* General Norms, article 2, 4 (*Origins* 20/17, p. 274); the other references are para. 12 (p. 268); para. 29 (p. 271); General Norms, article 2, 5 (p. 274). Paragraph 29 contains a representative statement of the entire document's approach to academic freedom, which I quote here: "The Church, accepting 'the legitimate autonomy of human culture and especially of the sciences,' recognizes the academic freedom of scholars in each discipline in accordance with its own principles and proper methods, and within the confines of the truth and the common good.

"Theology has its legitimate place in the university alongside other disciplines. It has proper principles and methods which define it as a branch of knowledge. Theologians enjoy the same freedom so long as they are faithful to these principles and methods."

50. "Instruction on the Ecclesial Vocation of the Theo-

logian," para. 1, (*Origins* 20/8, p. 117); para. 2 (p. 119); para. 3 (p. 119); para. 14 (p. 121); para. 20 (p. 122); para. 21 (p. 122); para. 35 (p. 124); para. 41 (p. 125).

51. "Instruction," para. 11, (*Origins* 20/8, p. 120); para. 12 (pp. 120–21).

52. "Instruction,"para. 32, (*Origins* 20/8, p. 123); para. 33 (p. 124).

53. *Ex Corde Ecclesiae* has 54 endnotes (*Origins* 20/17), pp. 275–76). Of the 54 notes, 35 are references to official church documents; all are concerned to secure the rights of authority or to establish the limits on what a Catholic university is to be and do. The "Instruction," Origins 20/8, 126, has 43 endnotes, 40 of which are references to church documents. All have the same purpose, to secure the rights of authority to establish effective limits on the freedom of the theologian.

54. Stanley Hauerwas, *A Community of Character* (Notre Dame, IN: University of Notre Dame Press, 1981), 72–86, has some interesting criticisms in this regard.

55. Leo XIII, *Rerum novarum* (On the Condition of Labor) 25–40, in *Seven Great Encyclicals* (Glen Rock, NY: Paulist Press, 1963), 15–25.

56. John XXIII, *Mater et magistra* (Christianity and Social Progress) 51–67, in Gremillion, 153–58. John quotes the principle itself from Pius XI in 53, Gremillion, p. 154.

57. National Conference of Catholic Bishops, *The Challenge of Peace: God's Promise and Our Response* 235–44 (Washington, DC: United States Catholic Conference, 1983), 73–76; *Economic Justice for All: Pastoral Letter on Catholic Social Teaching and the U.S. Economy* 295–325 (Washington, DC: United States Catholic Conference, 1986), 145–62.

58. Pius XI, *Quadragesimo anno* (Reconstructing the Social Order) 79, in *Seven Great Encyclicals*, 147.

59. *The Code of Canon Law*, 571–76, suggests that in the North American context, at least, most observers and most bishops agree that the bonds between church authority and Catholic colleges and universities are and should remain moral ones, not juridical ones, I am arguing here that this should be the case for more than economic and practical reasons.

60. The set of guidelines worked out in cooperation by committees of the Catholic Theological Society of America, the Canon Law Society of America and the bishops' Committee on Doctrine and approved by the National Conference of Catholic Bishops in June 1989, are a major step forward in recognizing the need for fair procedures and establishing practical guidelines for them. See, "Doctrinal Responsibilities: Ap-

proaches to Promoting Cooperation and Resolving Misunderstandings Between Bishops and Theologians," *Origins* 19/7 (29
June 1989), 97–110.

61. "Court Decision in Curran Case," *Origins* 18/40 (16
March 1989), 664–72, esp. V, 2, p. 671.

62. This was the point recognized in the 1940 AAUP statement in its exception clause for religious institutions. "Limitations of academic freedom because of religious or other aims
of the institution should be clearly stated in writing at the
time of appointment." See note 18.

63. Dulles, "The Teaching Mission of the Church and
Academic Freedom," 402.

Notes to Essay 2/Collins

1. Cf. Frans Neirynck, "Allan van Hoonacker et l'Index,"
ETL 57 (1981) 293–97.

2. In all, some 19 cardinals were involved in the effort to
censure Neirynck's work.

3. Cf. F.M. Stabile, "Il Cardinal Ruffini e il Vaticano II.
Le lettere di un 'intransigente,'" *Cristianesimo nella storia* 11
(1990) 83–176, p. 125. Neirynck's 61–page book under attack
was hardly more than a booklet (L'évangile de Noel selon Saint-
Luc [Brussels: La pensée catholique, 1970]).

4. Cf. my *Introduction to the New Testament* (Garden
City, NY: Doubleday, 1983) 376.

5. See Thomas S. Kuhn, *The Structure of Scientific Revo-
lutions* (Chicago: University Press, 1970).

6. Japan has a still smaller ratio, with but 11 lawyers per
100,000 population.

7. Cf. Dolores L. Christie, *Adequately Considered: An
American Perspective on Louis Janssen's Personalist Morals.*
Louvain Theological & Pastoral Monographs, 4. Louvain: Peeters,
1990–Grand Rapids: Eerdmans, 1991.

8. In the collegial system of our university, the rector
[president] of the university and deans of the various faculties
[schools] are elected by the teaching faculty and a proportionate number of assistants and students chosen by their peers.
Administrative responsibility of a given faculty [school] is
generally exercised by the *bureau*, an elected body, whose major decisions must be endorsed by the faculty board, that is,
the teaching faculty with a proportionate number of delegates
chosen from among the assistants and students of the faculty
[school].

9. Who is, so far as I know, no relation of the Louis Janssens mentioned above.

10. It is only in the phase of the doctoral dissertation that specialization takes place.

11. That is, especially the Roman Catholic church.

Notes to Essay 3/Dulles

1. Vatican Council II, *Gravissimum Educationis*, 3.

2. U.S. Bishops, *Human Life in Our Day* (Washington: USCC, 1968), 18–19.

3. James John Annarelli, *Academic Freedom and Catholic Higher Education* (Westport: Greenwood Press, 1987), 99, quotes Walter P. Metzger as stating: "The professional standing of a professor can only be established by experts, and these experts must be chosen from among his scholarly peers."

4. Annarelli, 102, quotes William J. Kilgore, chairman of a 1964 committee studying this question for the AAUP, as declaring that "each restriction [on academic freedom] might diminish the institution's academic effectiveness and standing." Kilgore adds such restrictions may reach a point at which the institution will "cease to be an institution of higher education according to the prevailing conception."

5. See Avery Dulles, "University Theology as a Service to the Church," *Thought* 64 (June 1984), 103–15.

6. John Henry Newman, *The Idea of a University* (Notre Dame: University of Notre Dame Press, 1982), Discourse IV, 53–74.

7. Annarelli, 206, asserts: "To establish limits that scholarly conclusions cannot transgress, or to impose an orthodoxy upon an entire university or particular department, is to contradict basic principles of academic freedom and to frustrate the exercise of the university's function."

8. "Doctrinal Responsibilities: Approaches to Promoting Cooperation and Resolving Misunderstandings between Bishops and Theologians," *Origins* 19:7 (June 29, 1989), 97–110; quotation from 102.

Notes to Essay 4/Wuerl

1. John Henry Newman, *The Idea of a University* (Notre

Dame: University of Notre Dame Press, 1982), Discourse II, no. 9.

2. Sidney Hook, *Heresy, Yes, Conspiracy, No,* (New York: John Day, 1953), 154.

3. Newman, *Essay on the Development of Christian Doctrine,* ch. 2, no. 2.

4. *Lumen Gentium,* 25.

5. Newman, *Essay,* ch. 5, sec. 1.

6. Pope John Paul II, speech in New Orleans, 12 Sept. 1987.

7. Newman, *Idea of a University,* Discourse IX, no. 2.

8. *Lumen Gentium,* 25.

9. Pope John Paul II, speech in New Orleans, 12 Sept. 1987.

Notes to Essay 5/Byron

1. John Henry Newman, *The Idea of A University* (Chicago: Loyola University of Chicago Press, 1927, reissued 1987) 5.

2. Newman, 28.

3. Newman, 30–31.

4. Newman, 246.

5. Robert Coles, *Simone Weil: A Modern Pilgrimage* (Reading: Addison-Wesley, 1987).

6. Newman, 450.

7. Newman, 451.

8. Newman, 452.

9. Newman, 453.

10. Newman, 453.

11. Newman, 455–56.

12. Cf. Rom. 12.2.

Notes to Essay 6/Curran

1. Neil G. McCluskey, ed., *The Catholic University: A Modern Appraisal* (Notre Dame, IN: University of Notre Dame Press, 1970).

2. The Catholic University of America, Self-Evaluation For the Middle States Association, January 1970.

3. Albert C. Pierce, *Beyond One Man* (Washington, DC: Anawim Press, 1967); Robert Townsend, "At The Cultural Crossroads of American Catholic Higher Education: The 1967

Strike At The Catholic University of America" (M.A. Dissertation, The Catholic University of America, 1990).

4. John F. Hunt, Terrence R. Connelly, *et al.*, *The Responsibility of Dissent: The Church and Academic Freedom* (New York: Sheed and Ward, 1967).

5. Resolution of the Board of Trustees of CUA, 2 June 1988.

6. Frederick H. Weisberg, Opinion and Order, CA 1562–87, *Curran v. Catholic University*, 28 February 1989. The full opinion is also published in *Origins* 18 (1989): 664–72; the quotation is found on 671.

7. "Reports: Seventy-Sixth Annual Meeting," *Academe: Bulletin of the American Association of University Professors* 76, n. 5. (Sept.–Oct. 1990), 28.

8. "Reports: Academic Freedom and Tenure: the Catholic University of America," *Academe: Bulletin of the American Association of University Professors* 75, n. 5 (Sept.–Oct. 1989), 27–40.

9. "Reports: Academic Freedom and Tenure," 29–32. See also my *Faithful Dissent* (Kansas City, Missouri: Sheed and Ward, 1986).

10. For a short, uncontested summary, see "Academic Freedom and Tenure CUA," *Academe: Bulletin of the American Association of University Professors* 75, n. 5 (Sept.–Oct. 1989), 27–28. For a complete history of CUA, see C. Joseph Nuesse, *The Catholic University of America: A Centennial History* (Washington, DC: Catholic University of America Press, 1990). See also John T. Ford, "'A Center of Light and Truth': A Century of Theology at the Catholic University of America," *The Catholic Historical Review* 85 (1989), 566–97. The briefs and court record in *Curran v. Catholic University* explain the positions of both parties in the dispute.

11. Bylaws of the University, June 1985, in "The Catholic University of America Faculty Handbook," (Washington, DC: 1980), 17–25.

12. Canonical Statutes for the Ecclesiastical Faculties of the Catholic University of America, 1981.

13. A transcript of the hearing was made—Before the Ad Hoc Committee in Re: Professor Charles Curran, 20 April, 4–6 May 1987.

14. Report to the Chancellor From the Ad Hoc Committee of the Academic Senate of the Catholic University of America in the Matter of Professor Charles E. Curran, 9 October 1987.

15. For a fuller explanation of this hearing and its aftermath,

see my *Catholic Higher Education, Theology, and Academic Freedom* (Notre Dame, IN: University of Notre Dame Press, 1990), 220–34.

16. Statement of the Board of Trustees of the Catholic University of America to the Ad Hoc Committee of the Academic Senate, sent under a cover letter from Cardinal Joseph Bernardin, Chair of the Board of Trustees, 27 January 1988.

17. Resolution of the Board of Trustees of the Catholic University of America, 2 June 1988.

18. Report to the Faculty, Administration, Trustees, Students of the Catholic University of America by an Evaluation Team Representing the Commission on Higher Education of the Middle States Association of Colleges and Schools, 34.

19. Origins (1989), 664–72.

20. Richard A. McCormick and Richard P. McBrien, "L'Affaire Curran II," *America* 163 (1990), 127–32+.

21. Auburn University Called Meeting of the University Senate, 15 January 1991, Resolution: Censure of President James E. Martin. See also "Auburn University: A Supplementary Report on a Censured Administration," *Academe: Bulletin of the American Association of University Professors* 77, n. 3 (May–June 1991), 34–40.

22. Deposition of William Franklin Baker in *Curran v. The Catholic University of America*, August 9, 1988; Deposition of Susan DeConcini in *Curran v. The Catholic University of America*, 9 September 1988.

23. E.g., Joseph O'Hare, "Faith and Freedom in Catholic Universities," in William W. May, ed., *Vatican Authority and American Catholic Dissent* (New York: Crossroads, 1987), 160–67.

24. Rodger Van Allen, "The Implications of the Curran Case for Academic Freedom," in May, *Vatican Authority and American Catholic Dissent*, 156–57.

25. "L'Affaire Curran: II," *America* 163 (1990), 127.

26. Pope John Paul II, *Ex Corde Ecclesiae: Apostolic Constitution on Catholic Universities* (Vatican City: Libreria Editrice Vaticana, 1990). The document is also published in *Origins* 20 (1990), 265–76.

27. James W. Sauve, "Pope John Paul II and Catholic Colleges and Universities," *America* 163 (October 1990): 260 ff; Charles E. Curran, "Point of View," *The Chronicle of Higher Education*, 30 January 1991, p. A 48.

28. "Editorial: A Charter for Catholic Universities," *America* 163 (1990), 259.

29. Archbishop Rembert Weakland, Press Conference, 12 November 1990.

30. "Point of View," *The Chronicle of Higher Education,* 30 January 1991, p. A 48.

31. E.g., Oscar H. Lipscomb, "Faith and Academic Freedom," *America* 159 (1988), 124–25; Daniel E. Pilarczyk, "Academic Freedom: Church and University," *Origins* 18 (1988), 57–59; Donald W. Wuerl, "Academic Freedom and the University," *Origins* 18 (1988), 207–11. In 1988 the bishops' conference in the United States generally supported the position of the Association of Catholic Colleges and Universities in objecting to some of the proposals in the proposed draft of the document on Catholic higher education. However, the congregation's summary indicates that seven individual American bishops strongly supported the proposed norms—Congregation for Catholic Education, "Summary of Responses to Draft Schema on Catholic Universities," *Origins* 17 (1988), 697. Note also that the episcopal trustees at Catholic University came out against academic freedom for that institution.

32. For my defense of academic freedom, see *Catholic Higher Education, Theology and Academic Freedom.*

Notes to Essay 7/Murray

1. Walter P. Metzger, *Profession and Constitution: Two Definitions of Academic Freedom in America,* Texas L. Rev. 66 (1988), 1265, 1269.

2. AAUP Policy Documents & Reports (1984 ed.), 3–4.

3. See e.g., Metzger, 1267. See also Richard P. McBrien, "Academic Freedom in Catholic Universities: The Emergence of a Party Line," *America* 159 (3 December 1988), 454.

4. Julius G. Getman & Jacqueline W. Mintz, *Foreword: Academic Freedom in a Changing Society,* Texas L. Rev. 66 (1988), 1247, 1249.

5. See Metzger, 1285.

6. Allan Bloom, *The Closing of the American Mind* (New York: Simon and Schuster, 1987).

7. Robert Nozick, *Philosophical Explanations* (Cambridge: Harvard UP, 1981) 629–30.

8. Nozick, 631.

9. Derek Curtis Bok, "Ethics, the University & Society," *Harvard Magazine* 39 (May–June 1988), 42.

10. Robert M. Hutchins delivered this paper as the Storrs

Lectures in 1935, and they were published under the title, *The Higher Learning in America* (New Haven: Yale UP, 1962), republished (Westport: Greenwood Press, 1979).

11. John Dewey, "President Hutchins' Proposals to Remake Higher Education," *The Social Frontier* (January 1937), as quoted in Harry S. Ashmore, *Unseasonable Truths: The Life of Robert Maynard Hutchins* (Boston: Little, Brown & Co., 1989), 163 (first emphasis supplied).

12. Mortimer J. Adler, *Philosopher at Large* (New York: Macmillan, 1977), 315, as quoted in Ashmore at 160.

13. Lon L. Fuller, *The Morality of Law* (New Haven: Yale UP, 1964).

14. Ronald M. Dworkin, *The Exclusive Morality of Law*, Villanova L. Rev. 10 (1965), 631.

15. See Nozick, 631 (footnote) where the author also suggests, "Indeed, since every theory will have defects, it is not enough to reject a theory on the basis of discerned flaws and inadequacies, especially if all one has to suggest in its place is something vague and ill-defined. For instance, 'communitarianism'"; see, for example, Roberto Unger, *Knowledge and Politics* (New York: Free Press, 1975).

16. John M. Finnis, *Natural Law and Natural Rights* (Oxford: Oxford UP, 1980).

17. McBrien, 455.

18. McBrien, 455.

19. Charles E. Curran, *Academic Freedom and Catholic Universities*, Texas L. Rev. 66 (1988), 1441, 1451.

20. Curran, 1453–454.

21. Curran, 1454.

22. See Douglas Laycock & Susan E. Waelbroeck, *Academic Freedom and the Free Exercise of Religion*, Texas L. Rev. 66 (1988), 1455, 1459.

23. This is the distinction suggested by Curran, 1452.

24. McBrien, 455.

25. Curran, 1452.

26. McBrien, 456.

27. McBrien, 456.

28. McBrien, 456.

29. See Laycock & Waelbroeck.

30. See McBrien.

31. James John Annarelli, Response, *Current Issues in Catholic Higher Education* 10, No. 1, (1989), 29 (responding to Father Byron's piece, "Discipline Inquiry: A Catholic Reflection on Academic Freedom" at 23).

32. Bishop Donald Wuerl, "Academic Freedom and the University," Newman Center, University of Massachusetts. 5 August 1988.

Notes to Essay 8/McBrien

1. There are various interpretations of academic freedom within the academy, the courts and the church. See Carl Peter, "The Many Faces of Academic Freedom," *Origins* 20/32 (17 January 1991), 520–24. Peter himself relies on Walter P. Metzger, "Profession and Constitution: Two Definitions of Academic Freedom in America," *Texas Law Review* 66/7 (1988), 1265–322, and Mark H. Yudof, "Three Faces of Academic Freedom," *Loyola Law Review* 32 (1987), 831–58. For a fuller treatment of the topic, see Charles E. Curran, *Catholic Higher Education, Theology and Academic Freedom* (Notre Dame, IN: University of Notre Dame Press, 1990).

2. It is not clear to me what Dr. John E. Murray, Jr., president of Duquesne University, means in his paper, "Symmetry Between Academic Freedom and a Catholic University," when he writes: "I am troubled by any suggestion that academic freedom can be limited by any external force in any discipline, including theology (in *Academic Freedom in a Pluralistic Society*, Nicholas P. Cafardi, ed.; Pittsburgh: Duquesne University, 1990, p. 50). This was in response to my concession that the academic freedom of the Catholic theologian" is limited by revelation and the teaching authority of the church. If a theologian wishes to be identified and recognized as a *Catholic* theologian, he or she cannot at the same time reject, for example, any doctrinally positive notion of Petrine ministry, of sacraments, of Real Presence, of the church as mystery, of the redemptive significance of the death and Resurrection of Christ, of eternal life, and so forth" (see my "Academic Freedom in Catholic Universities: The Emergence of a Party Line," *America* 159 [3 December 1988], 455).

I do not say that an outside, nonacademic agent can interfere with the academic freedom of a Catholic theologian in a Catholic university, but that a Catholic theologian's freedom *qua* Catholic theologian is limited. His or her faculty position and tenure would not be touched, but their right to be regarded as Catholic theologians would be. In other words, the Vatican, a national episcopal conference or even a diocesan bishop would have the right, in principle—and might even have the pastoral duty— to declare someone no longer a Catholic theologian, but that declaration would have no effect whatever on the theologian's faculty status within his or her institution of employment.

I regret that Dr. Murray devoted a substantial portion of his original symposium paper to a direct and explicit criticism of my view and those of Charles Curran ("Symmetry between Academic Freedom," pp. 48–50) when neither of us was invited to participate or given the opportunity to respond.

3. See, for example, Leonard A. Kennedy, "Academic Freedom and the Vatican: Will Catholic Universities Capitulate?" *Crisis* 4/10 (November 1986), 23–25; George A. Kelly, "The Catholic College: Death, Judgment, Resurrection," *Crisis* 5/3 (March 1987), 15–21; Sheldon Vanauken, "What Sort of Universities do Catholics Need?" *The Wanderer* 120/51 (17 December 1987), 4. Father Kennedy is a philosopher, Msgr. Kelly is a trained sociologist, and Dr. Vanauken is a professor of history and literature.

4. *Art. cit.*, 523.

5. These documents are available in American Association of University Professors, *Policy Documents and Reports* (Washington, DC: American Association of University Professors, 1984), 3–13. See also *Academe* 76 (May–June 1990), 37–44.

6. *Origins* 10/24 (27 November 1980), 380.

7. *Policy Documents and Reports*, 11. See also "The 'Limitations' Clause in the 1940 Statement of Principles," *Academe* 74 (Sept.–Oct. 1988), 52–57.

8. See Edward J. Power, *Catholic Higher Education in America: A History* (New York: Appleton-Century-Crofts, 1972); Philip Gleason, "American Catholic Higher Education: A Historical Perspective," in Robert Hassenger, ed., *The Shape of Catholic Higher Education* (Chicago: University of Chicago Press, 1967), 35–38; and Andrew M. Greeley, *From Backwater to Mainstream: A Profile of Catholic Higher Education* (New York: McGraw-Hill, 1969).

9. *Op. cit.*, 3.

10. *Op. cit.*, 35. For reasons why Catholics were opposed to academic freedom, see 54–62.

11. Cited in Curran, 78–79.

12. See Curran, 85–92.

13. For the full text, see *Origins* 15/43 (10 April 1986), 706–11.

14. "Catholic College and University Presidents Respond to Proposed Vatican Schema," *Origins* 15/23 (10 April 1986), 697, 699–704.

15. "Catholic College and University Presidents Respond," 703.

16. 155 (1 November 1986), 250.

17. "Rome and the Colleges: the Struggle for Autonomy," *Boston College Magazine* 48 (Summer 1989), 9.

18. "Catholic Higher Education," *Origins* 17/16 (1 October 1987), 268–70.

19. "Of Orthodoxy and Inquiry," *Boston College Magazine* 47 (Spring 1988), 49.

20. "Academic Freedom and the University," *Origins* 18/13 (8 September 1988), 207–11.

21. "Academic Freedom and the University," 208.

22. "Academic Freedom and the University," 209. It is of interest that Dr. Murray cites Bishop Wuerl's University of Massachusetts lecture in his final endnote, but does not take issue with the position advanced in the lecture. "Symmetry Between Academic Freedom," p. 54, n. 32.

23. The letter was published in *The Chronicle of Higher Education* 32 (2 April 1986), 26.

24. See, for example, Leo J. O'Donovan, ed., *Cooperation Between Theologians and the Ecclesiastical Magisterium: A Report of the Joint Committee of the Canon Law Society of America and the Catholic Theological Society of America* (Washington, DC: Canon Law Society of America 1982); and *Report of the Catholic Theological Society of America Committee on the Profession of Faith and the Oath of Fidelity* (Catholic Theological Society of America, 1990).

25. "The Teaching Mission of the Church and Academic Freedom," in Academic Freedom in a Pluralistic Society, 12. See also his "University Theology as a Service to the Church," *Thought* 64 (June 1989), 103–15.

26. "University Theology as a Service to the Church," 15.

27. "University Theology as a Service to the Church," 18.

28. "The Teaching Mission of the Church and Academic Freedom," 6.

29. "University Theology as a Service to the Church," 19.

30. "The Mandate to Teach Theological Disciplines: Glosses on Canon 812 of the New Code," *Theological Studies* 44 (1983), 488. See also his *The Church: Learning and Teaching* (Wilmington, DE: Michael Glazier, 1987), esp. 149–60, and "Magisterium and Theologians: A Vatican Document," *America* 163 (21 July 1990), 30–32.

31. "Canonical Mission and Catholic Universities," *America* 142 (7 June 1980), 476.

32. "Academic Freedom in Catholic Universities: The Emergence of a Party Line," *America* 159 (3 December 1988), 454–58.

33. "Academic Freedom in Catholic Universities: The Emergence of a Party Line," 454–55.

34. For full English-language text, see *Origins* 20/17 (4 October 1990), 265, 267–76.

35. For full English-language text, see "Instruction on the Ecclesial Vocation of the Theologian," *Origins* 20/8 (5 July 1990), 117, 119–26.

36. For the full text of the decision, see "Court Decision on Curran Case," *Origins* 18/40 (16 March 1989), 664–72, esp. 670–71.

37. "Court Decision on Curran Case," 671.

Notes to Essay 9/Worgul

1. F. Nietzsche "On the Truth and Lies in a Nonmoral Sense," in *Philosophy and Truth: Selections from Nietzsche's Notebooks of the Early 1870s* ed. D. Breazeale (N.J.: Humanities Press, 1979), 84.

2. D. Tracy, *Plurality and Ambiguity* (San Francisco: Harper and Row, 1987), 98.

3. cf. S.T. Coleridge, *Philosophical Lectures 1818–1819*, ed. K. Coburn (London, 1949) and *Aids to Reflection* (London, 1904).

4. cf. F.W.J. Schelling, "System des Transcendentalen Idealismus," *Werke*, ed. M. Schroter (Munchen, 1927), vol. 2.

5. cf, S.T. Coleridge, *Biographia Literaria*, ed. E. Rhys (London, 1906), 160–70.

6. cf. Goethe, *Werke* vol. 1 (Weimar, 1887–1930).

7. cf. M. Heidegger, *Being and Time* (N.Y. Harper and Row, 1927).

8. Heidegger, p. 15.

9. W. Naylor, *Daybread in the Dark Continent* (N.Y.: Young People's Missionary Movement of the United States and Canada, 1908), 148.

10. cf. *International Study Week on Mission and Liturgy: The Nijmegen Papers*, ed. J. Hofizer (N.Y.: P.J. Kennedy & Sons, 1960), 28.

11. *International Study Week on Mission and Liturgy*, p. 44.

12. *International Study Week on Mission and Liturgy*, p. 34.

13. P. Sarpong, "The Mission of the Local Church and the Inculturation of the Gospel," in *Mission and Dialogue* (N.Y.: Orbis Books, 1981), 540.

14. K. Pike "Etic and Emic Standpoints for the Description of Behavior," *Communication and Culture* ed. A. Smith (N.Y.: Holt, Reinhart and Winston, 1966), 152.

Index

175

About the Contributors

WILLIAM J. BYRON, S.J. is a priest-economist who has been president of The Catholic University of America since 1982. He previously served as the president of the University of Scranton and held a deanship at Loyola University of New Orleans. He earned his Ph.D. in economics from the University of Maryland. Dr. Byron is the author of *Quadrangle Considerations* (1989), which won the Catholic Press Association Best Book Award in the Education Category in 1990. In addition, he was nominated by President George Bush and confirmed by the U.S. Senate in July 1991 as a member of the Board of Directors for the Commission on National and Community Service.

RAYMOND F. COLLINS is professor of New Testament Studies at the Catholic University of Leuven in Belgium, and since 1990, he has served as chair of the Programs in English of the Faculty of Theology there. In 1971, he became the first American to be named to a tenured position since the foundation of the University in 1425. In addition to serving as editor in chief of *Louvain Studies*, he has authored seven books, including *Introduction to the New Testament* (1983), *Christian Morality: Biblical*

181

Foundations (1986) and *John and his Witness* (1991). Forthcoming publications include *The Birth of the New Testament* and *But I Say to You*. He is a priest of the diocese of Providence, Rhode Island.

CHARLES E. CURRAN is the Elizabeth Scurlock Professor of Human Values at Southern Methodist University. His many publications include *Catholic Higher Education, Theology, and Academic Freedom* (1990), *Tensions in Moral Theology* (1988), *Toward an American Catholic Moral Theology* (1987), *Directions in Catholic Social Ethics* (1985), *Directions in Fundamental Moral Theology* (1985) and *American Catholic Social Ethics: Twentieth-Century Approaches* (1984).

AVERY DULLES, S.J. is the Laurence J. McGinley Professor of Religion and Society at Fordham University. He is the author of 15 books, including *Models of the Church* (1974), *Models of Revelation* (1983), *The Catholicity of the Church* (1985) and *The Reshaping of Catholicism* (1988). His latest book is *The Craft of Theology: From Symbol to System* (1992). A past president of both the Catholic Theological Society of America and the American Theological Society, he serves as a consultor to the Committee on Doctrine of the National Conference of Catholic Bishops. He also received the Cardinal Spellman Award for distinguished achievement in theology. Dr. Dulles received his doctorate in Sacred Theology from the Gregorian University in Rome in 1960.

JAMES P. HANIGAN is professor of moral theology and director of graduate studies in the Theology Department at Duquesne University. His publications include *What Are They Saying About Sexual Morality* (Paulist Press, 1982), *As I Have Loved You: The Challenge of Christian Ethics* (Paulist Press, 1986) and *Homosexuality: The Test-Case for Christ Sexual Ethics* (Paulist Press, 1988). Dr. Hanigan earned his Ph.D. in religious studies from Duke University, and he presently serves as co-chair of the moral theology seminar for the convention of the Catholic Theological Society of America. In 1989, Dr. Hanigan was honored with the Presidential Award for Faculty Excellence in Scholarship at Duquesne.

RICHARD P. MCBRIEN, a priest of the Archdiocese of Hartford, Connecticut, is the Crowley-O'Brien-Walter Professor of Theology at the University of Notre Dame. He is the author of 15 books, including the Christopher Award-winning *Catholicism* (2 volumes; 1980–81), *Caesar's Coin: Religion and Politics in America* (1987), *Ministry: A Theological, Pastoral Handbook* (1987) and *Report on the Church: Catholicism Since Vatican II* (1992). A past president of the Catholic Theological Society of America, he received its John Courtney Murray Award for "outstanding and distinguished achievement in Theology" in 1976. He received his doctorate in Theology from the Pontifical Gregorian University in Rome.

JOHN E. MURRAY, JR. is president of Duquesne University. Before coming to Duquesne in 1988, Dr. Murray served as dean of the University of Pittsburgh and Villanova Schools of Law, and was Distinguished Professor of Law at the University of Pittsburgh. A nationally known legal scholar, Dr. Murray has written 11 books and numerous articles for many legal journals, as well as various articles on higher education and moral philosophy. For 11 years, he served as editor of the Journal of Legal Education, the official journal of the Association of American Law Schools. He earned his J.D. from the Catholic University of America and his S.J.D. from the University of Wisconsin.

GEORGE S. WORGUL, JR. is professor of systematic theology and chair of the Theology Department at Duquesne University. Dr. Worgul, who earned both his S.T.D. and his Ph.D. at the University of Louvain, is the author of *From Magic to Metaphor: A Validation of Christian Sacraments*. Dr. Worgul's research interests and publications center on ritual behavior and sacraments, ecclesiology and imagination; he has published over 30 articles both in this country and abroad.

DONALD W. WUERL is bishop of the Catholic Diocese of Pittsburgh. Bishop Wuerl is the author of *The Church and Her Sacraments: Making Christ Visible* (1990) and the coauthor of the widely used adult catechisms, *The Teaching of Christ* and *The Catholic Catechism*. He was elected as an honorary member of the Academia Romana for his writings on the history of the church in Rome. He earned his doctorate in theology from the Angelicum University in Rome. In 1990, he was appointed Distinguished Service Professor at Duquesne University.